PLAB

PART 1 EMQ

POCKET BOOK 1

PASTEST
Dedicated to your success

I would like to thank Dr Peter Kroker for his encouragement and support, Sam Lyon for helping me make sense and Helen for putting up with my long evenings in front of the computer!

PLAB

PART 1 EMQ

POCKET BOOK 1

Jonathan Treml

MB BS, BA, MRCP
Research Registrar,
Department for the Medicine of Ageing,
Chelsea and Westminster Hospital, London

PASTEST
Dedicated to your success

© 2000 PASTEST
Egerton Court, Parkgate Estate,
Knutsford, Cheshire, WA16 8DX
Telephone: 01565 752000

First edition 2000
Reprinted 2001, 2004

A catalogue record for this book is available from the British Library.

ISBN: 1 901198 56 1

The information contained within this book was obtained by the author from reliable sources. However, while every effort has been made to ensure its accuracy, no responsibility for loss, damage or injury occasioned to any person acting or refraining from action as a result of information contained herein can be accepted by the publishers or authors.

Typeset by Breeze Limited, Manchester
Printed by Cromwell Press Ltd, Wiltshire

CONTENTS

INTRODUCTION

About this book

Congratulations on buying this book!

Unfortunately, not everyone can pass PLAB Part 1 first time. At the time of writing, there are only a few books on the market that are designed to help you revise for the exam. Amazingly, many candidates do not buy any books or go on any courses. Whilst using this book, or any book, cannot guarantee a pass at the next exam, it will certainly improve your chances.

The proportion of candidates that pass is fixed at each sitting. Therefore, you are in competition with everyone that sits the exam the same time as you. If you help one of your friends with their revision, you may be helping them pass instead of you. Group learning is, of course, often of great benefit, but be careful that you are not helping others more than yourself. For your own sake, do not lend this book to anyone else until you have passed the exam…

This book is not a textbook. You will not find great detail and many topics could not be included in the space available. For revision, I would recommend that you use a small textbook or guide (such as the Oxford Handbook series). Subjects like paediatrics, obstetrics and psychiatry seem popular with the examiners. If you are weak in these areas, it might be worth obtaining small books dedicated to these specialities. Do not spend too much time or money on new, large textbooks. You will never read them.

This book is not, strictly speaking, a revision book. I have included very few lists in the text. Again, this is partly due to the limited number of topics that could be covered. Also, there are some very good books of lists and differential diagnosis already in print. If you like lists and your memory can cope with them, then it may be worth buying one of these books.

If you are new to the exam, this book will introduce you to the type of question that you will be facing. For those of you that have already sat the new exam (since July 2000), the book provides another 200 practice questions. Many difficult questions are made easier by understanding the way in which an examiner might think. I hope to provide some insight into the way in which the questions and answers are designed. This is particularly important now that the General Medical Council (GMC) has changed the format of the exam.

Introduction

The new exam and why it was changed

The General Medical Council (GMC) frequently reviews the way in which it examines overseas doctors in the PLAB process. Ultimately the exam may be replaced by another form of assessment. In the meantime, the GMC is keen to make the exam fairer and open to independent scrutiny. The previous Part 1 (multiple choice, picture and clinical problem-solving questions) was not felt to be a fair test of knowledge and ability.

A number of books were available for the previous model of exam. If you have any of these books, do not throw them away. The topics that are covered are still those that the PLAB exam will test. Incidentally, there is no guarantee that the exam format will not change again in the future.

Multiple choice questions (MCQs) are particularly subject to criticism. The new exam consists of Extended Matching Questions (EMQs), closely modelled on the style of exams in the USA. According to the GMC, the level of knowledge required to pass the new exam should be roughly the same as before. At the first sitting in July 2000, the exam was felt to be harder than expected by many candidates.

The GMC states that the standard required is that of a first year Senior House Officer, i.e. someone with 12 to 18 months experience since qualification. Some questions in July 2000 were almost certainly harder than that and seemed to expect greater depth of knowledge. Do not let this discourage you. A hard exam is equally hard on everyone. An easy exam is more likely to let weaker candidates pass by luck alone.

Many candidates in the July 2000 exam did not answer all 200 questions, you will need to practice using the time wisely. There will always be a few questions that you struggle with, try to waste as little time as possible on these. Put down an educated guess and move on quickly to a question you feel more confident about. This will boost your morale and produce greater time efficiency.

There were no picture questions in the July 2000 sitting of the Part 1 Exam and there will be no pictures in September. The GMC would not commit to whether picture questions will be reintroduced in the future.

Are EMQs harder than MCQs?

This is a difficult question to answer. MCQs are easy to set and mark. They test recall (often short term memory) and do not attempt to simulate clinical reality. A guess at multiple choice gives you a 50/50 chance of a correct answer. So does tossing a coin. An educated guess is often not much better due to the nature of the question. You either know it, or you don't.

EMQs are much harder to write. I have written over 1200 questions on about 250 themes in the last few months, so I should know! They test knowledge and deduction and often attempt to simulate clinical problem-solving. A random guess is unlikely to produce a correct answer when there may be as many as 14 possibilities. An educated guess is more likely to be right than wrong.

It is my opinion that EMQs are a better test of knowledge and experience. In clinical practice, if a 25-year-old man attends casualty with left-sided chest pain you do not think like this:

'Sudden unilateral chest pain in a 25-year-old man is commonly due to
> *pulmonary embolism – True*
> *pneumothorax – True*
> *dissecting thoracic aortic aneurysm – False'*

Whereas you might think the following:

'The most likely cause of sudden left-sided chest pain in a 25-year-old man is a pneumothorax'

EMQs also test the application of knowledge. In the July 2000 exam, most of the questions asked candidates to select the best investigation, rather than the most likely diagnosis. This is also relevant to clinical practice and harder to answer. When faced with the patient with chest pain, you will have a differential diagnosis and need to plan investigations to decide which diagnosis is correct. You may think the differential diagnosis is between pneumothorax, pulmonary embolism and oesophagitis. You must then decide whether a chest X-ray, arterial blood gases or an endoscopy is the investigation of choice. There may not be one single investigation that will establish the diagnosis in all circumstances, so you must pick the most discriminatory one. In this instance, a chest X-ray is probably the most useful test.

In answer to the question 'are EMQs harder than MCQs?', I would have to say the answer is probably 'Yes'. However, they are a better and fairer test of clinical ability. Doctors who pass this new exam will be those who have combined reading with hands-on experience. The previous Part 1 exam could, potentially, be passed by someone who had never seen a patient.

How to use this book

This book is designed as a complete mock PLAB Part 1 Examination. In the front section of this book there are 200 EMQs covering a wide selection of topics. The second section has answers to the questions with detailed, but not exhaustive, explanations to the answers. In the appendix, you will find a table of normal values for standard laboratory tests and a list of some drugs whose names or spellings are different in the UK to other countries.

I would suggest that you use the practice exam **under strict examination conditions**: make sure you set aside a full three hours for the exam, preferably during the daytime when the real exam will take place. Make sure you are not disturbed in any way – unplug the telephone, do not have any background music on and make sure your partner or flatmate is out of the way.

Work systematically through the exam paper from the beginning. Previous candidates found that some questions were considerably harder than others. If a question is obviously difficult, miss it out and move on to the next one. If the whole topic is unfamiliar to you, move on to the next one. Two minutes are more efficiently spent answering two easy questions than puzzling over one hard question. When you reach the end of the paper, go back to the questions you missed out until you run out of time. Three hours is not a long time to answer 200 questions, you have slightly less than one minute per question.

When the three hours have finished, stop answering questions. Relax and treat yourself, you deserve it!

When you are refreshed, come back and finish any questions you did not answer during the time on a separate sheet of paper. If you completed all 200 questions, well done! If not, have a go at all the others – an educated guess is often the right answer. Then go through the answers and mark the questions you managed during the time and see how you did. Look at the other questions separately. Use the explanations to identify areas of strength and weakness to guide your revision. It is difficult to say what score you will need to pass the exam, as the pass mark will vary at each sitting, depending on the difficulty of the exam. I would expect that a score of at least 50–60% would be a bare minimum to pass. In July 2000, the pass mark was 60% and the average mark was 58.5%.

It is unlikely that you will remember many of the questions in this book for long. About a week before the real thing, it will be worth trying this practice exam again. In using this book, you are making sure that the exam is not the first time you have encountered this type of question. Hopefully, the next PLAB Part 1 Exam will be the last one you have to take.

Good Luck!

Jonathan Treml

RECOMMENDED READING LIST

1. **Shorter Books which may be useful for Revision**

   Use **one** of these three:
   Lecture Notes on Clinical Medicine
   D Rubenstein and D Wayne, Blackwell Scientific Publications, 1997

   Oxford Handbook of Clinical Medicine
   R A Hope and J M Longmore, Oxford University Press, 1998

   Essential Medicine
   A E Read and J V Jones, Churchill Livingstone, 1998

   Both of these are also worth reading:
   Oxford Handbook of Clinical Specialities
   J A B Collier, J M Longmore and T J Hodgetts, Oxford University Press,
   4th edition 1995

   Essential Paediatrics
   D Hull and D I Johnston, Churchill Livingstone (also available as an
   International Student Edition)

2. **Books which are too long or detailed for revision but should be useful for reference**

   Acute Medicine
   D C Sprigings and J B Chambers, Blackwell Scientific Publications,
   2nd edition 1995.

   Medical Emergencies – Diagnosis and Management
   R Robinson and R B Stott, Butterworth Heinemann, 6th edition 1993

   Clinical Medicine
   P J Kumar and M L Clark, Balliere Tindall, 1998

   Textbook of Medicine
   R Souhami and J Moxham, Churchill Livingstone, 1997

   Lecture Notes on General Surgery
   H Ellis and R Calne, Blackwell Scientific Publications, 1998

Recommended Reading List

Handbook of General Surgery
P G Bevan and I A Donovan, Blackwell Scientific Publications, 1992

Concise System of Orthopaedics and Fractures
A G Apley and L Solomon, Butterworth Heinemann, 2nd edition 1994

Lecture Notes on Orthopaedics and Fractures
T Duckworth, Blackwell Scientific Publications, 3rd edition 1995

Lecture Notes on Gynaecology
G Chamberlain and J Malvern, Blackwell Scientific Publications, 1996

Gynaecology Illustrated
A D T Govan, C Hodge and R Callander, Churchill Livingstone, 4th edition 1993 (also available as an International Student Edition)

Lecture Notes on Obstetrics
G Chamberlain, M Pearce and P Hamilton, Blackwell Scientific Publications, 1996

Obstetrics Illustrated
A W F Miller and R Callander, Churchill Livingstone, 1997 (also available as an International Student Edition)

EMQ PRACTICE EXAMINATION

200 questions: time allowed 3 hours

Theme: Causes of constipation

Options

A	Poor fibre intake	G	Carcinoma of the rectum
B	Hypothyroidism	H	Carcinoma of the colon
C	Irritable bowel syndrome	I	Bowel obstruction
D	Hypercalcaemia	J	Pregnancy
E	Iatrogenic	K	Depression
F	Anal fissure	L	Bed rest

For each patient below, choose the SINGLE most likely diagnosis from the above list of options. Each option may be used once, more than once, or not at all.

1. A 40-year-old woman presents with a three-day history of constipation, colicky abdominal pain, distension and vomiting. She has not even passed wind. Bowel sounds are active and high-pitched.

2. A 30-year-old man complains of constipation and pain on defaecation. He also notices small amounts of fresh blood on the paper afterwards. He is unable to tolerate rectal examination.

3. A 21-year-old woman with mild learning difficulties complains of recent onset of abdominal distension, constipation, indigestion and amenorrhoea.

4. A 65-year-old man complains of constipation, low mood, low back pain that prevents him sleeping, fatigue and thirst. He has bony tenderness over his lumbar spine.

5. A 52-year-old woman complains of constipation and nausea four days after abdominal hysterectomy for fibroids. On examination she has active bowel sounds of normal pitch and pinpoint pupils.

6. A 60-year-old man presents with a two-month history of increasing constipation with occasional diarrhoea. He also describes anorexia, weight loss and a feeling of tenesmus.

Theme: Clinical signs of structural heart abnormalities

Options

A	Aortic stenosis	H	Ventricular septal defect
B	Aortic incompetence	I	Patent ductus arteriosus
C	Mitral stenosis	J	Mitral valve prolapse
D	Mitral incompetence	K	Pulmonary stenosis
E	Tricuspid regurgitation	L	Left ventricular aneurysm
F	Hypertrophic cardiomyopathy	M	Aortic sclerosis
G	Atrial septal defect	N	Tricuspid stenosis

For each list of clinical signs below, choose the SINGLE most likely diagnosis from the above list of options. Each option may be used once, more than once, or not at all.

7. There is a harsh pan-systolic murmur, loudest at the lower left sternal edge and inaudible at the apex. The apex is not displaced.

8. There is a soft late systolic murmur at the apex, radiating to the axilla.

9. The pulse is slow rising and the apex, which is not displaced, is heaving in character. There is an ejection systolic murmur heard best at the right second interspace that does not radiate.

10. The pulse is regular and jerky in character. The cardiac impulse is hyperdynamic and not displaced. There is a mid-systolic murmur, with no ejection click, loudest at the left sternal edge.

11. There is a constant 'machinery-like' murmur throughout systole and diastole. The patient is clubbed and cyanosed.

Theme: Prevention and treatment of thrombotic disease

Options

A	Aspirin	G	Intravenous heparin
B	Compression stockings	H	Warfarin (INR 2–3)
C	Early mobilisation	I	Warfarin (INR 3–4.5)
D	Foot pump	J	Phenindione
E	Subcutaneous unfractionated heparin	K	Thrombolysis
F	Subcutaneous low molecular weight heparin	L	Nothing

For each patient below, choose the BEST management from the above list of options. Each option may be used once, more than once, or not at all.

12. A 30-year-old woman is 16 weeks pregnant and develops a painful, swollen leg. A femoral vein thrombosis is diagnosed with Doppler ultrasound. She has already been started on intravenous heparin.

13. A 50-year-old man is admitted for an elective total hip replacement. He has a history of peptic ulcer disease and takes lansoprazole. He is otherwise well. What prophylaxis against thrombosis is indicated?

14. A 70-year-old man is in atrial fibrillation secondary to rheumatic mitral valve disease. Echocardiogram shows a dilated left atrium and mild mitral stenosis only. He has developed a severe rash with warfarin in the past.

15. A 22-year-old man is admitted for an elective haemorrhoidectomy. He has no other medical problems.

16. A 28-year-old woman has had four spontaneous abortions, two deep vein thromboses and suffers with migraine. Blood test confirms the presence of anti-cardiolipin antibodies.

17. A 30-year-old woman is 26 weeks pregnant and has collapsed at home, having had a painful swollen leg for two days. She is breathless and cyanosed despite receiving 60% oxygen via a facemask. Her pulse is 130/min, BP 80/40 mmHg. An urgent echocardiogram shows thrombus in the left pulmonary artery and evidence of right heart failure.

Theme: Planning and management of patients with head injury

Options

A	Admit for 24 hours observation	G	Intravenous dexamethasone
B	Discharge home	H	Transfer to neurosurgeons
C	Discharge home with advice	I	Skull X-rays
D	Urgent CT head	J	Intravenous mannitol
E	Immediate right-sided burr hole		
F	Immediate left-sided burr hole		

For each patient below, choose the BEST first step in management from the above list of options. Each option may be used once, more than once, or not at all.

18. A 25-year-old man hit his head on a plank in his garden. He did not lose consciousness and is alert and orientated with no focal neurological signs. He is complaining of a headache but has no other symptoms. He lives alone.

19. A 30-year-old woman tripped in the street and hit her head on a shop doorway. She thinks she briefly lost consciousness at the time. She has amnesia for about half an hour after the event but clearly remembers hitting her head. She lives with her husband.

20. A 45-year-old man slipped at an ice rink. He lost consciousness for five minutes. He does not recall falling but does remember skating with his children. He has a severe headache and some bruising around both eyes. There is clear liquid running from his left nostril which tests positive for glucose on dipstick.

21. A 3-year-old boy has a large fresh bruise on the side of his head. His father thinks that he fell off his swing in the garden. There are a number of bruises on both arms and legs. The boy refuses to talk and is uncooperative with examination. Skull X-rays show an old occipital fracture but no new fractures.

22. A 60-year-old man was hit by a car as he crossed the road. He has sustained injuries to his head and both lower legs. One hour after the injury, he is drowsy and will not open his eyes. He extends his limbs and makes noises to painful stimuli. His right pupil is fixed and dilated. Pulse is 60/min and BP is 180/120 mmHg. The nearest neurosurgical centre with an empty bed is over two hours away. The CT scanner at your hospital is being repaired.

23. A 42-year-old homeless man is brought in to casualty by the police. He was found wandering the streets claiming to have been assaulted. He denies any loss of consciousness. He has a large scalp laceration over his occiput. He is alert and orientated and has no focal neurological signs. He smells strongly of alcohol.

Theme: Prescribing for patients in renal failure

Options

A	No changes required	E	Relatively contraindicated
B	Reduce dose	F	Higher doses may be needed
C	Reduced dose frequency	G	Monitor drug levels more often
D	Absolutely contraindicated		

For each drug below, choose the CORRECT advice from the above list of options. Each option may be used once, more than once, or not at all.

24. Captopril in moderate renal impairment

25. Gentamicin in severe chronic renal impairment

26. Frusemide (furosemide) for pulmonary oedema in severe acute renal failure

27. Phenytoin in severe renal impairment

28. Cefalexin in severe chronic renal impairment

Theme: Investigation of urinary tract symptoms

Options

A	Urine microscopy	G	Flexible cystoscopy
B	Urine microscopy and culture	H	Barium enema
C	KUB X-ray	I	Prostate specific antigen
D	Renal tract ultrasound	J	Blood glucose
E	Urodynamic studies	K	Serum calcium
F	Urine cytology	L	Urethral swab culture

For each patient below, choose the MOST USEFUL diagnostic test from the above list of options. Each option may be used once, more than once, or not at all.

29. A 25-year-old woman was admitted two days ago with high fevers, rigors and left loin pain. She has received six doses of intravenous Cefuroxime. Urine culture has grown a coliform organism, which is sensitive to cephalosporins. Her loin pain is getting worse and she continues to spike very high fevers.

30. A 30-year-old man complains of sharp pain on passing urine. He has also noticed a thin discharge after micturition. He has a number of sexual partners and does not use condoms.

31. A 65-year-old carpenter complains of urinary frequency and urgency, fatigue and thirst. He has lost one stone in weight over the past three months.

32. A 58-year-old tyre-factory worker has noticed a number of episodes of fresh haematuria. He has no pain on passing urine and otherwise feels well.

33. A 68-year-old woman presents with a short history of passing foul urine with green-brown discoloration. She has also noticed bubbles in her stream of urine. She was treated for carcinoma of the cervix in the past.

Theme: Investigation of acute abdominal pain

Options

A	Serum amylase	G	Diagnostic peritoneal tap or lavage
B	White cell count	H	CT abdomen ± contrast
C	C reactive protein	I	Diagnostic laparoscopy
D	Abdominal ultrasound	J	β HCG
E	Erect chest X-ray	K	Gastrografin enema
F	Supine abdominal X-ray	L	Immediate laparotomy

For each patient below, choose the investigation of FIRST choice from the above list of options. Each option may be used once, more than once, or not at all.

34. A 25-year-old woman presents in a state of collapse. She has a painful, tender, rigid abdomen. Pulse is 120/min, BP 80/50 mmHg. Bowel sounds are scanty.

35. A 52-year-old man presents with onset of severe abdominal pain over an hour. He has a history of episodic epigastric pain over the last three months. He is afebrile, tachycardic and normotensive. He has generalised tenderness with guarding, and absent bowel sounds.

36. A 42-year-old obese woman complains of a 24-hour history of severe epigastric pain and profuse vomiting. On examination she is tachycardic and mildly jaundiced. She has mild tenderness in the left upper quadrant and normal bowel sounds.

37. A 45-year-old builder fell from scaffolding to the ground this evening. He landed on his left side and initially had pain in his left lower chest. He has now developed severe abdominal pain. He is becoming increasingly tachycardic and is hypotensive. His abdomen is tender with guarding and he is tender over his left 10th and 11th ribs.

38. A 70-year-old woman has developed an increasingly painful and swollen abdomen over a period of 24 hours. She has not opened her bowels for three days and has begun to vomit today. On examination she has a distended, tender abdomen with scanty bowel sounds. She has an exquisitely tender mass at the top of her right thigh.

39. A 70-year-old man presents with sudden severe central abdominal pain and collapse. He is severely shocked. He has a tender, rigid abdomen and there is an expansile, pulsatile mass in the upper abdomen.

Theme: Symptoms and signs of normal pregnancy

Options

A	4 weeks	F	2nd trimester
B	8 weeks	G	3rd trimester
C	12 weeks	H	Any time during pregnancy
D	16 weeks	I	Not part of normal pregnancy
E	20 weeks		

For each clinical feature below, choose the MOST likely stage of pregnancy from the above list of options. Each option may be used once, more than once, or not at all.

40. Morning sickness begins

41. Fetal movements felt for the first time in a mother's third pregnancy

42. Low back pain, worse at night

43. Nipples are enlarged and begin to darken

44. Polycythaemia

Theme: Immediate investigation of unconscious patient

Options

A	Blood glucose	G	CT brain
B	Arterial blood gases	H	Lumbar puncture
C	Toxicology screen	I	Electroencephalogram
D	ECG	J	Blood alcohol
E	Chest X-ray	K	No investigations, treat immediately
F	Serum amylase	L	No investigations, admit for observation

For each patient below, choose the investigation of FIRST choice from the above list of options. Each option may be used once, more than once, or not at all.

45. A 30-year-old man collapsed at a night-club. He has a Glasgow Coma Score of 3. He has evidence of neck stiffness. His pulse is 60/min and his BP is 170/100 mmHg.

46. A 60-year-old man was brought into casualty complaining of chest pain. His ECG at that time was normal and he is awaiting the results of blood tests. After two hours, he suddenly complains of feeling very faint and collapses. His BP is barely recordable and his pulse is very weak.

47. A 21-year-old woman collapsed at a party. Her friends say that she had drunk several bottles of beer before acting strangely for about half an hour prior to collapsing. She has been incontinent of urine. On examination she is clammy, sweaty and tachycardic.

48. A 24-year-old man with asthma has become increasingly breathless over the last three hours. He also had left-sided chest pain. He has now collapsed and is cyanosed and tachypnoeic. Pulse 120/min, BP 90/60 mmHg. His trachea is deviated to the right and his apex beat is impalpable.

49. A 19-year-old man is admitted to casualty unconscious. The paramedics report that he was witnessed to have a grand mal seizure in a cafe. It is not known whether he has a history of epilepsy or any other medical illness. Capillary blood glucose performed in the ambulance was 18 mmol/l.

Theme: Interpretation of haematological results

Options

A	β Thalassaemia minor	G	Folate deficiency
B	Cytotoxic drugs	H	B12 deficiency
C	Rheumatoid arthritis	I	Acute myeloid leukaemia
D	Alcoholic liver disease	J	Chronic myeloid leukaemia
E	Myelodysplasia	K	Chronic lymphocytic leukaemia
F	Iron deficiency	L	Old age

For each set of results below, choose the SINGLE most likely diagnosis from the above list of options. Each option may be used once, more than once, or not at all.

50. 40-year-old woman: Hb 9.0 g/dl, MCV 82 fl, WCC 8.1 x 10^9/l, platelets 450 x 10^9/l. Serum ferritin 300 mg/l.

51. 50-year-old man with longstanding epilepsy: Hb 10.1 g/dl, MCV 115 fl, WCC 3.8 x 10^9/l (lymphocytes 2.5, neutrophils 1.3), platelets 243 x 10^9/l.

52. 21-year-old woman, booking visit to ante-natal clinic: Hb 9.7 g/dl, MCV 71 fl, MCH 27 pg, red cell count 6.7 x 10^{12}/l, WCC 6.4 x 10^9/l, platelets 310 x 10^9/l, HbA2 5%.

53. 75-year-old woman, investigations for fatigue: Hb 9.4 g/dl, MCV 102 fl, WCC 4.5 x 10^9/l (lymphocytes 1.8, neutrophils 1.7, monocytes 1.0, myeloblasts 0.1), platelets 190 x 10^9/l.

54. 60-year-old man, routine blood test: Hb 10.8 g/dl, MCV 87 fl, MCH 30 pg, WCC 18.4 x 10^9/l, platelets 190 x 10^9/l. Direct antiglobulin test – positive.

55. 55-year-old man, routine blood test: Hb 13.8 g/dl, MCV 106 fl, WCC 6.7 x 10^9/l, platelets 110 x 10^9/l. Blood film – target cells and hypersegmented neutrophils.

Theme: Over-the-counter medications

Options

A	Paracetamol	H	Topical clotrimazole
B	Aspirin	I	Xylometazoline nasal spray
C	Loperamide	J	Sodium cromoglycate nasal spray
D	Cimetidine	K	Aluminium hydroxide/magnesium trisilicate
E	Chlorpheniramine		
F	Loratadine	L	Malathion lotion
G	1% hydrocortisone ointment	M	Should be investigated first

For each patient below, choose the SINGLE most appropriate medication from the above list of options. Each option may be used once, more than once, or not at all.

56. A 24-year-old woman complains of vulval itching and a white vaginal discharge.

57. A 30-year-old man complains of heartburn, indigestion and reflux with waterbrash.

58. A 3-year-old girl is febrile and irritable with a generalised vesicular rash. She has a history of a febrile convulsion in the past.

59. A 21-year-old student suffers with hay fever. He is due to take his final exams and is worried that the hay fever will affect his performance. However, he is also worried that medication may make him drowsy.

60. A 54-year-old man has a two-month history of epigastric pain after meals.

Theme: Headache - selection of diagnostic tests

Options

A	CT head	F	Cervical spine X-ray
B	MRI brain	G	Sinus X-ray
C	Lumbar puncture	H	Skull X-ray
D	ESR	I	No tests required
E	Temporal artery biopsy		

For each patient below, choose the MOST important investigation from the above list of options. Each option may be used once, more than once, or not at all.

61. A 59-year-old woman presents with severe left-sided headache for three days. She has no past history of note. Her left temporal artery is tender and pulseless.

62. A 24-year-old woman complains of headaches every four weeks. She started taking the oral contraceptive pill four months ago and her headaches are getting worse. The headaches last up to two days and she is unable to work during that time.

63. An 18-year-old man presents with a 24-hour history of severe right frontal headache and nasal congestion. He is tender over his right forehead.

64. Three days ago, a 40-year-old builder was hit by a plank while he was at work. He did not lose consciousness at the time and has no amnesia, he vomited once. He is now complaining of increasing headache, dizziness and poor concentration. He says that he is worried about returning to work.

65. A 35-year-old woman complains of increasing headache over a two-month period. The headache is worse in the morning and on bending forwards. She has also noticed some difficulty in writing but had put this down to being distracted by the headache.

66. A 20-year-old man complains of a severe generalised headache and photophobia for two days. He has a low-grade fever, sore throat and mild neck stiffness. He has no neurological signs or rashes.

Theme: Prescribing for pain relief

Options

A	Paracetamol	G	Morphine
B	Aspirin	H	Diamorphine
C	Co-proxamol	I	Nitrous oxide
D	Ibuprofen	J	Pethidine
E	Diclofenac	K	Carbamazepine
F	Tramadol	L	Topical ketoprofen

For each patient below, choose the MOST appropriate treatment from the above list of options. Each option may be used once, more than once, or not at all.

67. A 12-year-old boy has just had a dental extraction and is complaining of a painful jaw.

68. A 70-year-old woman has bone pain from metastatic breast cancer. Simple analgesia has been ineffective.

69. A 35-year-old man is admitted with an acutely painful abdomen. He has epigastric tenderness. His amylase is elevated.

70. A 65-year-old man has an acutely painful, red and swollen left knee. He has recently been started on frusemide by his GP.

71. A 50-year-old woman has severe shooting pains in the left side of her face following an attack of shingles. She has tried a number of painkillers from the local pharmacy without benefit.

72. A 21-year-old man has dislocated the terminal phalanx of his left little finger in a fight. There does not appear to be a fracture and you wish to give him analgesia to allow reduction of the dislocation.

Theme: Management of diabetes mellitus

Options

A	Metformin	H	Twice-daily long/short mixed insulin
B	Acarbose		injections
C	Glibenclamide	I	One long- and three short-acting insulin
D	Gliclazide		injections
E	Repaglinide	J	Intravenous insulin sliding scale
F	Dietary adjustment	K	Subcutaneous insulin sliding scale
G	Once-daily long- acting insulin injection	L	No change in treatment required

For each patient below, choose the NEXT management step from the above list of options. Each option may be used once, more than once, or not at all.

73. A 78-year-old woman was diagnosed with diabetes after she was found to have a high blood glucose during an admission to hospital with a fall. Despite following appropriate dietary advice, her HbA1c remains elevated at 11%. She is visually impaired and finds it impossible to test her blood glucose at home. She is not obese.

74. A 27-year-old woman was found to have glycosuria at a routine antenatal clinic visit. A glucose tolerance test confirmed the diagnosis of gestational diabetes.

75. A 65-year-old man has had type 2 diabetes for four years, for which he was taking chlorpropamide. He presents with an acute myocardial infarction and his laboratory blood glucose is 11 mmol/l.

76. A 58-year-old man was diagnosed with diabetes at a routine medical three months ago. His body mass index is 32 despite losing 5 kg by following the dietician's advice. His home blood glucose readings range from 7 to 11 and his HbA1c is 10%.

77. A 32-year-old woman has had type 1 diabetes for 15 years. She injects isophane insulin twice a day and rarely tests her blood glucose at home. She attends the diabetic clinic for the first time in over a year and informs you that she is 12 weeks pregnant.

78. A 65-year-old man has had type 2 diabetes for at least five years. He is on the maximum dose of tolbutamide and metformin. All his home blood glucose readings are greater than 11 mmol/l and he has symptoms of thirst and weight loss. His body mass index is 22.

Theme: Causes of vaginal bleeding

Options

A	Normal menstruation	G	Exogenous oestrogens
B	Cervical polyps	H	Ectopic pregnancy
C	Cervical carcinoma	I	Spontaneous abortion
D	Cervical ectropion	J	Bleeding disorder
E	Atrophic vaginitis	K	Foreign body
F	Endometrial carcinoma		

For each patient below, choose the SINGLE most likely diagnosis from the above list of options. Each option may be used once, more than once, or not at all.

79. A 20-year-old woman has a very heavy period and passes several clots. Her last period was 45 days ago. She normally has a regular 30-day cycle with light periods. She is otherwise well.

80. A 22-year-old woman has been on the oral contraceptive for six months. She has developed intermenstrual and postcoital bleeding. Speculum examination shows the visible part of the cervix to be red.

81. A 78-year-old woman has had treatment for a uterine prolapse. She has recently developed vaginal bleeding which is increasing in severity. She is frail but otherwise well. Uterine curettage reveals no histological abnormality.

82. A 34-year-old woman presents with dark vaginal bleeding. Prior to this she has had colicky left iliac fossa pain for a few days. She has a history of pelvic inflammatory disease and irregular periods.

83. A 55-year-old post-menopausal woman has developed post-coital bleeding. She also describes dyspareunia and urinary stress incontinence.

Theme: Management of drug dependency

Options

A	Disulfiram	G	Chlormethiazole
B	Methadone	H	Chlordiazepoxide
C	Needle exchange programme	I	Naloxone
D	Intravenous vitamin B and thiamine	J	Group psychotherapy
E	Gradual reducing course of diazepam		
F	Outpatient referral to drug dependency team	K	Inform police
		L	Hospital admission

For each scenario below, choose the management of FIRST choice from the above list of options. Each option may be used once, more than once, or not at all.

84. A 70-year-old woman has taken 20 mg of temazepam at night for the last 30 years. She has begun to suffer with falls and has agreed that the temazepam might be contributing to the falls.

85. A 26-year-old heroin addict is worried because her partner has been diagnosed as having HIV infection. She is HIV negative. She does not feel able to stop using heroin at the present time.

86. A 40-year-old man has become increasingly dependent on alcohol since his wife died last year. He admits that he has a problem and wishes to stop drinking. He does not wish to take anti-depressants.

87. A 30-year-old builder was admitted for an elective anterior cruciate ligament repair. He admits to drinking at least 60 units of alcohol per week and has no desire to stop. You are keen to prevent him from developing a withdrawal syndrome as this may impair his recovery from the operation.

88. A 63-year-old retired surgeon is admitted with a short history of bizarre behaviour. He claims that the GMC are investigating him for murder and have hired a private detective to follow him. He has evidence of a coarse tremor, horizontal nystagmus and an ataxic gait. His wife says that the story about the GMC is untrue but is worried about the amount of gin that her husband has drunk since retirement.

89. A 37-year-old retired professional footballer admits to using cocaine and heroin for the last three years. He has recently signed a contract to present a sports show on television and wishes to 'clean his life up' first. His wife and family are very supportive of this.

Theme: Advice for travellers - vaccinations

Options

A	No precautions required	F	Hepatitis A, typhoid and polio vaccines
B	Hepatitis A vaccine only		
C	Typhoid vaccine only	G	Hepatitis A and B, typhoid, polio, diphtheria and rabies vaccines
D	Typhoid and polio vaccines only		
E	Rabies vaccine only	H	All of G and yellow fever also
		I	All of H and meningitis (a and c) also

For each traveller below, choose the CORRECT advice from the above list of options. Each option may be used once, more than once, or not at all. Assume each patient is currently resident in the UK.

90. A doctor is travelling to Somalia to work for the International Red Cross.

91. A businessman is going to a conference in Thailand.

92. A 40-year-old man intends to travel to Barbados for a holiday. He had hepatitis A four years ago and received polio vaccine as a child.

93. A 12-year-old girl is travelling to rural France with her parents.

Theme: Management of complications of pregnancy

Options

A	Urgent Caesarean section	G	Warfarin
B	Oral methyldopa	H	Heparin
C	Intravenous labetalol	I	Induction of labour
D	Intravenous fluids	J	Admit for monitoring
E	Blood transfusion	K	High concentration oxygen
F	Oral antibiotics	L	No treatment required

For each patient below, choose the management of FIRST choice from the above list of options. Each option may be used once, more than once, or not at all.

94. A 28-year-old woman is eight weeks pregnant with her first child. She has severe vomiting and is unable to keep food or fluids down. She has lost 3 kg in the last week. Her skin turgor is low. Urinalysis reveals ketones and a trace of blood and protein but no nitrites.

95. A 32-year-old woman is 34 weeks pregnant with her fourth child. She has not had any antenatal care. She presents with sudden massive vaginal blood loss preceded by a couple of smaller bleeds. She has no abdominal pain or tenderness. Pulse is 110/min, BP 80/30 mmHg and the fetal heart rate is 140/min.

96. A 40-year-old pregnant woman had an amniocentesis at 16 weeks, as she was concerned about the risk of Down's syndrome. 12 hours later she collapsed at home. She is breathless and cyanosed. She has had a generalised convulsion and is developing a purpuric rash. Pulse is 100/min, BP 100/50 mmHg.

97. A 26-year-old woman is 27 weeks pregnant with her first child. She is complaining of aching of both lower legs, which are swollen. She is also suffering with crampy pains in her left calf at night. On examination there is symmetrical pitting oedema of both calves with no tenderness of either calf. BP is 90/40 mmHg and she has no proteinuria.

98. A 17-year-old woman is in the 25th week of her first pregnancy and is attending a routine antenatal clinic. Her pulse is 110/min and BP is 150/90 mmHg. There is proteinuria on urine dipstick.

99. A 36-year-old woman is 34 weeks pregnant with her third child. She has recently received treatment to correct a breech presentation. Recent ultrasound showed the placenta to be lying in a normal position. She has collapsed with severe lower abdominal pain and has lost around 100 ml blood vaginally. Her pulse is 120/min and BP is 80/50 mmHg. The fetal heart rate is 80/min.

Theme: Prescribing in pregnancy

Options

A	Avoid in all trimesters	F	Avoid in more than one trimester
B	Avoid in first trimester		
C	Avoid in second trimester	G	No restrictions
D	Avoid in third trimester	H	Continue treatment if already started
E	Avoid just prior to delivery		

For each drug below, choose the CORRECT advice from the above list of options. Each option may be used once, more than once, or not at all.

100. Lisinopril

101. Warfarin

102. Phenytoin

103. Trimethoprim

104. Glibenclamide

Theme: Causes of respiratory symptoms in children

Options

A	Asthma	G	Diphtheria
B	Acute bronchiolitis	I	Inhaled foreign body
C	Croup	J	Tracheo-oesophageal fistula
D	Pneumonia	K	Cystic fibrosis
E	Whooping cough	L	Cardiac disease
F	Epiglottitis	M	Respiratory distress syndrome

For each patient below, choose the SINGLE most likely diagnosis from the above list of options. Each option may be used once, more than once, or not at all.

105. A two-year-old girl has been unwell for two months with difficulty breathing. She has a barking cough with no sputum. The cough is worse at night and after feeding. Sometimes the bouts of coughing end with vomiting. There is no wheeze.

106. A three-year-old boy has had a chronic cough for three months. He has had several chest infections and has required several courses of antibiotics. On examination he has a monophonic wheeze heard in the right lower lung field. He is systemically well.

107. A six-year-old refugee from Chechnya is unwell with a high fever, sore throat and harsh cough. She has some difficulty swallowing and has a hoarse voice. There is a thick grey exudate on the tonsils.

108. A five-month-old girl has been tired and irritable for a few days with a runny nose. She now has a cough and is wheezy. On examination her temperature is 37.8 °C and she has nasal flaring, intercostal recession and cyanosis.

109. A one-month-old baby has had a chronic cough since birth and has been treated for two episodes of pneumonia. He becomes cyanosed when feeding. He is on the 3rd centile for weight despite abdominal distension. When coughing, he produces copious amounts of secretions and appears to 'blow bubbles'.

Theme: Causes of pre- and perinatal infections

Options

A	*Toxoplasma gondii*	G	Group B streptococcus
B	Herpes simplex	H	*Listeria monocytogenes*
C	Herpes zoster	I	*Chlamydia trachomatis*
D	Rubella	J	*Escherichia coli*
E	Cytomegalovirus		
F	Human immunodeficiency virus		

For each syndrome described below, choose the MOST likely cause from the above list of options. Each option may be used once, more than once, or not at all.

110. This child was initially quite well and was on the 50th centile for weight. From eight months, however, she failed to thrive and rapidly fell to the 3rd centile over the next three months. She had severe diarrhoea, recurrent episodes of fever and breathing difficulties. On examination, she has generalised lymphadenopathy and eczema.

111. This child has moderate learning difficulties, cerebral palsy and growth delay. There was prolonged jaundice after birth. There is also severe visual impairment due to choroidoretinitis. The mother was unaware of any illness during pregnancy.

112. This child was well for the first week after birth before rapidly deteriorating. He now refuses to feed, is drowsy and has had apnoea attacks and fits. On examination he appears very unwell and shocked with evidence of neck stiffness.

113. This child developed a blistering rash on his scalp and face 10 days after birth. The conjunctivae are also red and blistered. He has jaundice and hepatomegaly.

114. This child developed a purulent discharge of both conjunctivae eight days after birth. On examination there are no corneal ulcers or retinal changes. He was otherwise well, initially, but has now developed a cough, fever and cyanosis.

Theme: Choice of treatment for arrhythmias

Options

A	Carotid sinus massage	G	Lignocaine
B	Adenosine	H	Calcium chloride
C	Verapamil	I	Flecainide
D	Sotalol	J	Disopyramide
E	Amiodarone	K	Elective DC cardioversion
F	Digoxin	L	Emergency DC cardioversion

For each patient below, choose the BEST first step in management from the above list of options. Each option may be used once, more than once, or not at all.

115. A 30-year-old woman has a six-month history of palpitations. Her resting ECG shows a shortened PR interval and delta waves. Holter monitoring reveals evidence of paroxysmal supraventricular tachycardia.

116. A 50-year-old man was admitted with an acute anterior myocardial infarction earlier today. Two hours after completion of thrombolysis with TPA, he suddenly complains of feeling faint. His pulse is 140/min and BP is 90/40 mmHg. His cardiac monitor shows long runs of ventricular tachycardia.

117. A 24-year-old woman presents to casualty complaining of dizziness. Her ECG shows re-entry tachycardia. She had one similar episode in the past, which stopped spontaneously, and she is on no medication. She is 31 weeks pregnant.

118. A 70-year-old man has collapsed on a surgical ward following a left hemicolectomy. He has a very weak carotid pulse. His BP is unrecordable. Cardiac monitor shows a broad complex tachycardia with a rate of 160/min.

119. A 60-year-old man has chronic renal failure, which is treated with continuous ambulatory peritoneal dialysis. He has had a low-grade fever and abdominal pain for the last two days and he has noticed that the dialysate is cloudy after exchange. He is receiving attention in casualty when he suddenly becomes unwell with a broad complex tachycardia. His BP is 80/50 mmHg.

Theme: *Management of hyperlipidaemia*

Options

A	No specific treatment required	G	Cholestyramine
B	Statin	H	Nicotinic acid
C	Fibrate	I	Treat secondary cause first
D	Fibrate and statin		
E	Diet: Fat intake < 30% of calories, with < 10% as saturated fat		
F	Diet: Fat intake < 25% of calories, with < 7% as saturated fat		

For each patient below, choose the treatment of FIRST choice from the above list of options. Each option may be used once, more than once, or not at all. Where a drug is recommended, you should assume that dietary advice is also given.

120. A 60-year-old woman has recently diagnosed type 2 diabetes and is found to have a fasting total cholesterol level of 4.9 mmol/l and triglyceride of 4.0 mmol/l. After six months of dietary treatment, her diabetes is well controlled but her triglyceride is still 3.8 mmol/l.

121. A 70-year-old man has suffered an acute inferior myocardial infarction. He is found to have a total cholesterol level of 5.0 mmol/l and triglyceride of 2.5 mmol/l on discharge from hospital.

122. A 40-year-old woman has symptomatic primary biliary cirrhosis. Her total cholesterol is 7.8 mmol/l and triglyceride is 2.1 mmol/l.

123. A 35-year-old man was admitted with acute pancreatitis. After recovering from this, he was found to have a triglyceride level of 7.4 mmol/l. His cholesterol is 6.7 mmol/l. He admits to drinking four cans of strong lager every day.

124. A 52-year-old man has peripheral vascular disease and angina. He has no secondary causes for dyslipidaemia. His total cholesterol is measured as 5.8 mmol/l and his triglyceride level is 3.4 mmol/l.

Theme: Choice of contraception

Options

A	Rhythm methods	F	Post-coital high-dose
B	Barrier methods		levonorgestrel
C	Progesterone-only pill	G	Intra-uterine contraceptive
D	Combined oral contraceptive		device
E	Progesterone depot injection	H	Vasectomy
		I	Laparoscopic sterilisation

For each patient below, choose the MOST appropriate management from the above list of options. Each option may be used once, more than once, or not at all.

125. A couple have had three children and are both sure that they have completed their family. The wife does not wish to take the oral contraceptive, as she is concerned about the possible risks, and they are not keen on using condoms. Both are aged 35.

126. A 25-year-old shift worker wishes to avoid pregnancy for at least the next six months. She suffers with regular classical migraines. Her partner has a latex allergy.

127. A 38-year-old married woman has had two children and would like reliable contraception. She is not absolutely sure that she and her husband will not want a third child at some stage.

128. A 21-year-old woman had unprotected intercourse at a party two days ago. She does not wish to become pregnant.

129. A 26-year-old Catholic couple attend their GP's surgery asking about contraception. The wife suffers with irregular periods that are painful and heavy.

130. A 28-year-old woman has discovered that her partner has been using intravenous heroin. She wishes to continue a sexual relationship with him.

Theme: Interpretation of tests of respiratory disease

Options

A	Asthma	G	Pulmonary haemorrhage
B	Emphysema	H	Extrinsic allergic alveolitis
C	Chronic bronchitis	I	Pneumonectomy
D	Pulmonary fibrosis	J	Pulmonary embolism
E	Panic attack	K	Sarcoidosis
F	Cystic fibrosis	L	Extrinsic tracheal compression

For each set of results below, choose the MOST likely diagnosis from the above list of options. Each option may be used once, more than once, or not at all.

131. 30-year-old woman: Arterial blood gases – pH 7.51, pCO_2 3.7 kPa, pO_2 14.3 kPa, HCO_3^- 28 mmol/l.

132. 40-year-old Afro-Caribbean woman: Lung function tests – FEV_1 2.5 l, FVC 2.9 l, FEV_1/FVC 86%. Serum ACE – high.

133. 60-year-old male non-smoker: Lung function tests – FEV_1 1.4 l, FVC 3.5 l, FEV_1/FVC = 40%. After bronchodilator trial – FEV_1/FVC = 50%. After two weeks of Prednisolone 30 mg daily – FEV_1/FVC = 65%.

134. 50-year-old farmer: Lung function tests – FEV_1 2.8 l, FVC 3.5 l, FEV_1/FVC = 80%. Reduced TLCO and KCO. Bronchoalveolar lavage – lymphocytes and mast cells. Precipitins to Micropolyspora faeni – positive.

135. 35-year-old woman: Arterial blood gases – pH 7.40, pCO_2 4.4, pO_2 9.4. TLCO 90% of predicted, KCO 160% of predicted. All results were normal 24 hours ago.

Theme: Diagnosis of common congenital diseases in children

Options

A	Blood film	G	Karyotyping
B	Haemoglobin electrophoresis	H	Genetic testing
C	Direct and indirect bilirubin	I	Echocardiography
D	Sweat test	J	Immunoglobulin levels
E	Heel-prick (Guthrie) test	K	Specific enzyme levels
F	Urinary homocysteine	L	Clinical diagnosis only, no diagnostic test

For each patient below, choose the SINGLE most useful investigation from the above list of options. Each option may be used once, more than once, or not at all.

136. A week-old baby is permanently sleepy and floppy and rarely feeds or cries. He has an excessively large tongue and is jaundiced, bradycardic and hyporeflexic.

137. A three-year-old girl is admitted with painful swellings of her hands and feet. She had prolonged jaundice after birth but has developed normally. On examination she has splenomegaly and is jaundiced and pale.

138. A four-year-old boy has had recurrent chest infections since birth and has now developed intermittent diarrhoea. He is failing to gain weight or height normally. A recent sputum culture grew *Staph. aureus.*

139. A 14-year-old girl has not yet begun to menstruate. She gets teased for being the shortest girl in her class. On examination she has delayed breast development with wide-spaced nipples. There is a systolic murmur heard at the left sternal edge.

140. A 12-year-old boy had a protracted attack of gastro-enteritis during which he became jaundiced. Now both the jaundice and gastro-enteritis have settled. His mother says that he became jaundiced as a younger boy when he had a chest infection.

141. A 20-month-old girl has failed to thrive since soon after birth. She is very pale and appears breathless. She has frontal bossing of the skull and splenomegaly.

Theme: *Management of lower limb fractures*

Options

A	Traction	H	Open reduction and internal fixation
B	Below-knee plaster		
C	Above-knee plaster	I	External fixation
D	Dynamic hip screw	J	Dynamic condylar screw
E	Intramedullary nail	K	Bed rest only
F	Hemi-arthroplasty	L	Analgesia and active mobilisation
G	Total hip replacement		

For each patient below, choose the DEFINITIVE management from the above list of options. Each option may be used once, more than once, or not at all.

142. A 78-year-old woman is admitted with an intertrochanteric fracture of her proximal femur. She has dementia and cardiac failure, which is reasonably well controlled. She lives in a nursing home and usually uses a Zimmer frame to walk short distances.

143. An 84-year-old man is admitted with a painful left hip after a fall at home. He has a fracture of his left inferior and superior pubic rami but his femur appears intact. He has pain on standing. He has no significant medical history.

144. An obese 32-year-old woman tripped on the kerb with eversion of her right foot. She has a displaced fracture of the medial malleolus and fracture of the fibula above the level of the tibio-fibular joint.

145. A 14-year-old boy fell from a stolen moped and sustained an open comminuted fracture of the distal third of his femur.

146. A 64-year-old woman with a history of osteoporosis is admitted with a displaced sub-capital fracture of the right femoral neck. She has no other medical problems and is usually mobile without walking aids.

Theme: Management of renal failure

Options

A	Intravenous fluids	H	Calcium gluconate
B	Fluid restriction	I	Calcium resonium
C	Haemodialysis	J	Venesection
D	Haemofiltration	K	Intravenous dopamine
E	Peritoneal dialysis	L	Intravenous frusemide
F	Insulin and dextrose	M	Intravenous nitrate
G	Urinary catheter		

For each patient below, choose the MOST important step in management from the above list of options. Each option may be used once, more than once, or not at all.

147. A 64-year-old woman receives continuous peritoneal dialysis for chronic renal impairment due to hypertensive nephropathy. She is on no medications likely to cause hyperkalaemia but her potassium level is persistently in the range 6.0 – 6.4 mmol/l. She does not feel unwell and her ECG is normal.

148. A 72-year-old man is admitted with increasing breathlessness and anuria for three days. His clinical signs are consistent with pulmonary oedema with small pleural effusions. He has a distended abdomen, which is dull to percussion between the umbilicus and symphysis pubis. His potassium is 5.9 mmol/l, urea is 62 mmol/l and his creatinine is 1100 μmol/l.

149. A 36-year-old man presents with a one-week history of breathlessness, haemoptysis and oliguria. He has widespread crackles and wheezes in his chest. He has a pericardial rub and third heart sound. Potassium is 5.5 mmol/l, urea is 53 mmol/l, creatinine is 620 μmol/l. His chest X-ray shows pulmonary oedema, bilateral pleural effusions and diffuse peripheral infiltrates. Urinalysis reveals red cells and casts. ECG shows widespread ST elevation. You have full renal facilities available in your hospital.

150. A 42-year-old woman had a hysterectomy three days ago for fibroids. Since the operation she has been vomiting profusely and is now complaining of thirst and malaise. Sodium is 148 mmol/l, potassium 3.1 mmol/l, urea is 24 mmol/l and creatinine is 118 μmol/l. Her pre-operative blood tests were normal.

151. A 51-year-old man presents with severe breathlessness. Clinically, he is in severe pulmonary oedema (confirmed on chest X-ray) and looks moribund. His ECG shows no acute changes. His potassium is 5.5 mmol/l, urea 48 mmol/l, creatinine 520 μmol/l. He has received two intravenous boluses of 100 mg frusemide with no improvement in his clinical condition. His BP is 80/40 mmHg despite intravenous dopamine. No urine has been passed since he was catheterised. Your ITU has no beds and cannot provide haemofiltration. The nearest renal unit with a vacant bed is over two hours away.

Theme: Side-effects of medications

Options

A	Amiodarone	G	L-Dopa
B	Aspirin	H	Lisinopril
C	Atenolol	I	Lithium
D	Carbimazole	J	Metformin
E	Chlorpromazine	K	Sulphasalazine
F	Erythromycin	L	Verapamil

For each list of side-effects below, choose the MOST likely causative agent from the above list of options. Each option may be used once, more than once, or not at all.

152. Cold hands and feet, fatigue, impotence.

153. Peripheral neuropathy, pulmonary fibrosis, hyperthyroidism.

154. Postural hypotension, involuntary movements, nausea, discoloration of the urine.

155. Thirst, polyuria, tremor, rashes, hypothyroidism.

156. Sore throat, rash, pruritus, nausea.

Theme: Causes of clubbing

Options

A	Squamous cell lung cancer	H	Crohn's disease
B	Mesothelioma	I	Infective endocarditis
C	Cystic fibrosis	J	Cyanotic congenital heart
D	Bronchiectasis		disease
E	Fibrosing alveolitis	K	Hyperthyroidism
F	Coeliac disease	L	Axillary artery aneurysm
G	Hepatic cirrhosis		

For each patient below, choose the MOST likely cause of clubbing from the above list of options. Each option may be used once, more than once, or not at all.

157. A 74-year-old man is admitted with fever and breathlessness. He recently had a trans-urethral resection of the prostate but was otherwise well until three weeks ago. On examination, his temperature is 37.7 °C, his pulse is 96/min and regular, and his BP is 180/80 mmHg. He has an early diastolic murmur. His chest is clear. He has blood on urine dipstick. He has evidence of early clubbing.

158. A 27-year-old woman suffers with recurrent chest infections and has a chronic productive cough. She remembers having had whooping cough as a child. On examination, she is not febrile or cyanosed but has marked clubbing. She has widespread crackles, wheezes and clicks on auscultation of her chest, which do not clear with coughing.

159. A 68-year-old man presents with a three-month history of cough and weight loss. On examination, he is cachectic. He has a hyper-expanded, quiet chest with no abnormal breath sounds heard. He has left-sided ptosis and bilateral clubbing. He recently stopped smoking and gives a history of asbestos exposure in the 1980s.

160. A 15-year-old boy is under investigation for weight loss. He gives a history of intermittent abdominal pain and diarrhoea. His stools are often pale and hard to flush away. On examination, he is thin and pale-skinned with fair hair but with no specific abnormalities apart from clubbing.

161. A 53-year-old man has clubbing in the left hand only. He has a history of hypertension and angina, with three-vessel coronary disease shown on angiography two years ago. His hypertension and angina are well controlled on medication.

Theme: Advice for travellers – malaria prophylaxis

Options

A	No precautions required	E	Doxycycline only
B	Chloroquine only	F	Proguanil and chloroquine
C	Mefloquine only	G	Maloprim and chloroquine
D	Proguanil only		

For each traveller below, choose the CORRECT advice from the above list of options. Each option may be used once, more than once, or not at all. Assume each patient is currently resident in the United Kingdom.

162. A sports fan is travelling to Jamaica for a three-week cricket holiday.

163. A young backpacker is planning to travel through Thailand and Western Cambodia.

164. A Ghanaian, who is now resident in London, is returning to Ghana for a month's holiday. He has had malaria in the past.

165. A student is travelling to Kenya for a two-week holiday. He has a history of manic depression but is currently taking no medication.

Theme: Investigation of lumps in the neck

Options

A	Ultrasound	G	Thyroid function tests
B	Technetium scan	H	Doppler ultrasound
C	Iodine uptake scan	I	Digital subtraction angiography
D	Fine needle aspiration	J	Sialogram
E	Excision biopsy	K	Nasopharyngoscopy
F	Paul Bunnell test		

For each patient below, choose the MOST discriminatory investigation from the above list of options. Each option may be used once, more than once, or not at all.

166. A 53-year-old woman presents with a six-month history of a mass below the angle of the jaw on the right. It is gradually increasing in size and is mobile and firm to the touch. There is no associated pain or facial weakness.

167. A 68-year-old man presents with a mass in the anterior triangle of the neck. It has increased in size over the last two months. It is soft, pulsatile and has an associated bruit.

168. A 38-year-old woman presents with a two-month history of a swelling in the anterior part of the neck, left of the midline. The swelling is not painful and she feels otherwise well. On examination, she has a solitary thyroid nodule in the left lobe of the thyroid. She is clinically euthyroid.

169. A 46-year-old woman presents with a diffuse swelling in the anterior part of the neck. She also describes a hoarse voice. On examination, she has a diffuse multinodular goitre, bradycardia and slow-relaxing reflexes.

170. A 27-year-old man describes intermittent painful swelling below his jaw. The pain and swelling is worse on eating. He is otherwise well. On examination, there is a small, tender swelling in the left submandibular region.

171. A 72-year-old man presents with a hard, painless swelling in the anterior triangle of the neck. He has had a hoarse voice for two months. He is a lifelong smoker and drinks heavily.

Theme: Investigation of hyperventilation

Options

A	No investigation required	G	Urea and electrolytes
B	Chest X-ray	H	Blood glucose
C	Salicylate levels	I	Serum lactate
D	CT brain	J	Blood count and film
E	Spiral CT chest with contrast	K	Echocardiogram
F	Arterial blood gases	L	Ventilation-perfusion scan

For each patient below, choose the SINGLE most discriminatory investigation from the above list of options. Each option may be used once, more than once, or not at all.

172. A 26-year-old nurse is brought into casualty as an emergency. She is hyperventilating but drowsy. She has been complaining of nausea and tinnitus and had an episode of haematemesis in the ambulance.

173. A 21-year-old motorcycle courier was involved in a head on collision with a van. He had an obvious deformity of his left thigh and knee. X-ray confirmed a comminuted fracture of the shaft of the femur that was reduced and placed in traction. Five days later, he suddenly deteriorates; he becomes drowsy, confused and febrile. He is hyperventilating and cyanosed. There are crackles at both lung bases and petechiae over his chest and neck.

174. A 15-year-old schoolgirl was out with her friends at a party last night. When she returned home this morning, she was drowsy, unwell and vomiting. She has lost 5 kg over the last two months. On arrival at hospital, she is drowsy, confused and hyperventilating but not cyanosed. Her breath smells of pear drops.

175. A 24-year-old car mechanic is brought to casualty by his girlfriend. She describes a two-day history of rigors, sweats and intermittent confusion. On examination, he is agitated, sweaty and pyrexial with a temperature of 38.6 °C. He is hyperventilating and cyanosed despite receiving oxygen by facemask. There is dullness to percussion and bronchial breathing at the left lung base.

176. A 14-year-old boy presents to casualty complaining of severe chest pain and difficulty breathing. He is hyperventilating and pale but not cyanosed. He has had four similar admissions in the last year and his older brother also attends hospital frequently.

177. A 29-year-old teacher is seven months pregnant. She presents with sudden collapse and breathlessness. On examination, she is afebrile, severely cyanosed and hyperventilating. Her pulse is 140/min and BP is 70/30 mmHg.

Theme: Warnings for specific drugs

Options

A	Must be taken with food	G	Take with a full glass of water at least 30 minutes before breakfast and remain upright until after breakfast
B	Must be taken on an empty stomach		
C	Must avoid alcoholic drinks	H	May reduce effect of contraceptive
D	This drug may colour the urine		
E	Not to be stopped without doctor's advice	I	May cause blue-tinted vision
		J	Not to be taken with antacids
F	Avoid exposure of the skin to direct sunlight	K	Not to be taken with iron tablets

For each medication below, choose the BEST advice from the above list of options. Each option may be used once, more than once, or not at all.

178. Sulfasalazine

179. Chlorpropamide

180. Sildenafil

181. Alendronate

182. Ampicillin

Theme: Causes of hepatomegaly

Options

A	Congestive cardiac failure	H	Chronic lymphocytic
B	Tricuspid regurgitation		leukaemia
C	Malaria	I	Acute myeloid leukaemia
D	Infectious mononucleosis	J	Lymphoma
E	Hepatocellular carcinoma	K	Myelofibrosis
F	Liver metastases	L	Amyloidosis
G	Chronic myeloid leukaemia		

For each patient below, choose the SINGLE most likely diagnosis from the above list of options. Each option may be used once, more than once, or not at all.

183. A 20-year-old student presents to her GP with a one-week history of fever and sore throat. On examination, she has tender cervical lymphadenopathy and an enlarged, tender liver.

184. A 62-year-old man presents with a three-month history of intermittent constipation and diarrhoea and progressive weight loss. On examination, he is cachectic and has knobbly hepatomegaly. He is not jaundiced. His liver function tests are normal.

185. An 81-year-old woman presents with a six-month history of abdominal swelling, hepatomegaly and leg oedema. She has a past history of rheumatic fever as a child and hypertension for the last few years. She takes atenolol for her hypertension.

186. A 56-year-old woman has a 20-year history of rheumatoid arthritis. Despite numerous drugs, her arthritis has only recently come under control. Recently she has noticed that she bruises easily. On examination she has a large beefy tongue, lymphadenopathy and hepatomegaly.

187. A 31-year-old man presents to casualty with a two-week history of night sweats, weight loss and pruritus. He has noticed some enlarged glands in his groin that are painful if he drinks alcohol. On examination he has no other evidence of lymphadenopathy and a smooth enlarged liver.

Theme: Causes of pulmonary oedema

Options

A	Myocardial infarction	G	Constrictive pericarditis
B	Myocarditis	H	Iatrogenic
C	Cardiomyopathy	I	Hypoalbuminaemia
D	Mitral regurgitation	J	Adult respiratory distress syndrome
E	Mitral stenosis	K	Anaemia
F	Aortic stenosis	L	Acute renal failure

For each patient below, choose the MOST likely diagnosis from the above list of options. Each option may be used once, more than once, or not at all.

188. A 74-year-old woman presents to casualty with acute breathlessness. She has had three similar admissions in the last few months. She has a past history of rheumatic fever. On examination, she has an irregular pulse of 110/min. She has a non-displaced, tapping apex beat with no evidence of left ventricular dysfunction. No murmurs are audible. There are crepitations heard in both lower lung fields.

189. A 67-year-old man has had an elective total knee replacement. He has no significant medical history. 36 hours after the operation, he complains of increasing breathlessness. He is cyanosed and has crackles up to the mid-zones of both lungs. His ECG is normal and chest X-ray shows pulmonary oedema with normal cardiac dimensions. His urine output since the operation has been poor and he has been persistently hypotensive with a BP around 90/60 mmHg.

190. A 21-year-old man has become increasingly breathless over a period of four days. He has also had severe central chest pain and a fever. He was previously fit and well. On examination, he looks unwell, cyanosed and dyspnoeic. Pulse is 120/min regular, BP 90/40 mmHg, JVP is elevated and he has a gallop rhythm with no murmurs. There are crackles in both lung bases. Chest X-ray shows pulmonary oedema and a normal heart size. ECG shows extensive ST elevation in the anterior and inferior leads without Q waves.

191. A 38-year-old woman was admitted to hospital two days ago with abdominal pain and vomiting. She was tender in the epigastrium and was found to have a very high serum amylase level. She has been treated with large volumes of intravenous fluids and has maintained a good urine output. Nonetheless she has been persistently hypoxic and is deteriorating rapidly. She now has crackles throughout both lung fields and a pO_2 of 5.1 kPa despite receiving 60% O_2 by mask. Chest X-ray shows massive bilateral pulmonary oedema. Her serum albumin is 30 mmol/l.

Theme: Treatment of psychiatric disease

Options

A	Amitriptyline	G	Diazepam
B	Phenelzine	H	Temazepam
C	Fluoxetine	I	Zopiclone
D	Buspirone	J	Risperidone
E	Lithium carbonate	K	Thioridazine
F	Haloperidol	L	Drug treatment not appropriate

For each patient below, choose the MOST appropriate treatment from the above list of options. Each option may be used once, more than once, or not at all.

192. A 28-year-old woman lost her job as a secretary three months ago. She attends her GP's surgery complaining of difficulty sleeping. She feels tired all the time, has a poor appetite and has lost some weight. She says she feels worthless and is helpless to do anything about it. She says that before she was fired from her job her boss had been recording her phone calls and that sometimes she heard him telling her colleagues that she was the worst person he had ever hired. She has thought about committing suicide and says that her husband 'would not miss her if she was dead'.

193. A 41-year-old man has been brought to casualty after being found in the street acting in a bizarre fashion. He was exposing his genitals to passers-by and shouting 'I am the salvation of the world'. In casualty, he is very angry and agitated and wants to return to the streets to complete his missionary work. He refuses to have any tests in hospital and says 'the devil will punish you for interfering in his work'.

194. A 21-year-old single woman gave birth to her first child two days ago. Since the birth she has been unable to sleep and is reluctant to hold her baby or feed her. She is very tearful and cries for no reason. She denies any thoughts of harm for herself or her baby. She had been looking forward to having a baby, even though she had no regular partner and was not sure of the identity of the father. She lives with her parents.

195. A 64-year-old woman has a three-year history of increasing confusion, loss of mobility and tremor. She has recently developed frequent visual hallucinations and tends to cry out for no reason, particularly at night. There is no evidence of an acute medical cause for her confusion. On examination she is alert but disorientated and quite agitated. She has a coarse resting tremor, increased tone in her limbs and normal reflexes.

Theme: Investigation of malignant disease

Options

A	Prostate-specific antigen (PSA)	G	Incision biopsy
B	Alpha-fetoprotein (AFP)	H	Excision biopsy
C	Carcino-embryonic antigen (CEA)	I	Ultrasound
D	CA 19-9	J	CT scan
E	Chest X-ray	K	Mammogram
F	Cytology	L	Endoscopic examination

For each patient below, choose the investigation of FIRST choice from the above list of options. Each option may be used once, more than once, or not at all.

196. A 42-year-old woman has noticed a lump in her left breast. There is a strong family history of breast cancer, which affected her mother and sister. There has been no pain in the breast or discharge from the nipple. On examination, she has generally lumpy breasts, but says that one particular lump is new and increasing in size.

197. A 23-year-old man has developed a swelling in his scrotum over a three-month period. It is firm and painless and arises from the left testicle. He has a history of asthma and orchidopexy.

198. A 68-year-old man presents with a one-year history of urinary frequency and post-micturition dribble. He has a medical history of atrial fibrillation and takes warfarin. On examination, he has an enlarged prostate with an irregular surface and loss of the medial sulcus.

199. A 55-year-old woman had a left hemicolectomy two years ago for a carcinoma of the sigmoid colon. Histology was reported as showing tumour invasion through the muscularis mucosa. She has recently developed a change in bowel habit with no weight loss or rectal bleeding. Abdominal examination is normal.

200. A 72-year-old woman has a six-month history of abdominal swelling and malaise. On examination, there is generalised abdominal distension with shifting dullness and the suggestion of a pelvic mass. She is on warfarin for a pulmonary embolism.

EMQ PRACTICE EXAMINATION – ANSWERS AND EXPLANATIONS

Theme: Causes of constipation

1. **I**

   Absolute constipation (i.e. inability to pass flatus as well as faeces) is one of the cardinal features of bowel obstruction. The other features are colicky abdominal pain, distension and vomiting. In small bowel obstruction, constipation appears after the onset of vomiting; in large bowel obstruction, vomiting appears later. High-pitched bowel sounds are strongly suggestive of mechanical bowel obstruction. Functional obstruction (pseudo-obstruction) may cause a similar clinical picture but the bowel sounds are often absent.

2. **F**

   Anal fissure is a very common problem and often follows a period of relative constipation. The passage of a hard stool produces a fissure, the pain of which causes anal spasm and further constipation. The resultant vicious cycle is broken with stool softeners and local anaesthetic preparations. Topical nitrates have also proved useful in reducing spasm. Severe cases may require an anal stretch or lateral sphincterotomy under anaesthetic.

3. **J**

   Pregnancy causes constipation due to the presence of a pelvic mass and due to reduced gastro-intestinal motility. Indigestion occurs later as smooth muscle relaxation reduces the tone of the gastro-oesophageal sphincter and results in acid reflux. Pregnancy in young women may present late, even in the absence of learning difficulties.

4. **D**

   The combination of depression, fatigue, constipation and bone pain is suggestive of hypercalcaemia. In a man of this age, the likely cause is malignant disease. Back pain that prevents sleeping is also suspicious for metastases or myeloma. Hypothyroidism could explain most of the symptoms apart from back pain. Colorectal carcinoma does not commonly produce bone metastases.

5. **E**

Patients in hospital often develop constipation for a number of reasons including pain, poor fluid intake, lack of dietary fibre, immobility and medication. It would be unlikely that a routine hysterectomy would result in bowel obstruction directly. However, it is very likely that opiate analgesia, given for post-operative pain, will cause constipation if adequate fluids, fibre and/or laxatives are not provided. Nausea may be due to impending bowel obstruction or due directly to the opiates. Pinpoint pupils also suggest the patient is receiving excess opiates.

6. **G**

Tenesmus, the feeling that the bowel is incompletely emptied after evacuation, is a symptom that is associated with rectal tumours (carcinoma or polyps) and irritable bowel syndrome. It is unusual for irritable bowel syndrome to develop in a patient of older age and the presence of anorexia and weight loss is more consistent with cancer.

Theme: Clinical signs of structural heart abnormalities

This question tests basic clinical knowledge. Most of the answers are self-explanatory.

7. **H**

    The amplitude of a murmur depends on the amount of turbulence or flow. A small VSD (maladie de Roger) is louder than a large one. With a small VSD the pressure in the left ventricle is higher than the right so there is high flow per cross sectional area of the defect. In a large VSD, ventricular pressures may equalise and there will be no flow across the defect. Reversal of the direction of flow (i.e. a right to left shunt) may occur precipitating cyanosis and breathlessness. This is Eisenmenger's syndrome and may occur acutely or chronically.

8. **J**

    Late systolic murmurs that otherwise resemble mitral incompetence are usually due to mitral valve prolapse but may also be due to mild mitral incompetence (usually secondary to prolapse in such cases). There may also (or only) be a mid-systolic click. Clinical identification is important, as most cardiologists advise endocarditis prophylaxis for patients with mitral valve prolapse if it is clinically apparent but not if it is an echo-only diagnosis.

9. **A**

    This is the classical description of aortic stenosis. As the gradient increases the murmur gets louder and the pulse pressure lower. There may also be postural hypotension. As the left ventricle fails, however, the murmur becomes softer as the flow through the valve is reduced.

10. **F**

    This is a classical description of hypertrophic cardiomyopathy. The hypertrophic septum causes functional obstruction of the left ventricular outflow tract (sub-aortic stenosis) and produces a murmur similar to aortic stenosis except that the second heart sound is normal.

11. **I**

    Patent ductus arteriosus is now almost always identified and treated in the neonatal period. The murmur, when heard, is usually characteristic.

Theme: Prevention and treatment of thrombotic disease

This is a potentially controversial area!

Warfarin is generally used for prolonged treatment or prophylaxis of thromboembolic disease. Therapeutic ranges for INR (International Normalised Ratio) are:

Treatment of PE or above-knee DVT	INR 2.0–3.0 for 3–6 months
Recurrent DVT or PE	INR 3.0–4.5 for life
DVT or PE due to anti-phospholipid antibodies	INR 3.0–4.5 for life
Metallic prosthetic heart valve	INR 3.0–4.5 for life
Rheumatic atrial fibrillation	INR 2.0–3.0 for life
Atrial fibrillation and mitral valve disease, hypertension, dilated left atrium or age >75	INR 2.0–3.0 for life

Uncomplicated non-rheumatic atrial fibrillation in patients aged <75 and other AF patients with contraindications to warfarin should receive aspirin.

Guidelines for thrombo-prophylaxis in surgical practice are not universal. Subcutaneous heparin remains in common use. Low molecular weight heparins are increasingly used, particularly in orthopaedic practice, due to a lower incidence of bleeding complications. In addition, mechanical methods, such as foot pumps, compression stockings and early mobilisation, are beneficial and should be recommended in appropriate circumstances.

Where warfarin is contraindicated, heparin is usually appropriate. Where a patient has a documented allergy to warfarin, which is rare, other anti-coagulants (phenindione and nicoumalone) may be used.

continues…

continued…

12. H

A pregnant woman may receive warfarin in the second trimester in relative safety. DVT is best diagnosed with Doppler ultrasound, to avoid the use of ionising radiation near the fetus.

13. F

Previous peptic ulcer disease is a contraindication to aspirin but not to anti-coagulation. Active bleeding, however, is a relative contraindication to anti-coagulation. Low molecular weight heparin has been shown to reduce the incidence of DVT in elective orthopaedic patients without a significant increase in bleeding complications.

14. J

Rheumatic atrial fibrillation is an indication for anti-coagulation. Phenindione may be used in the context of a documented warfarin allergy.

15. B

A young patient is at low risk of DVT unless he has pelvic or lower limb surgery. The risk of bleeding or haematoma formation after haemorrhoidectomy is high. Mechanical prophylaxis is probably of benefit and TED (Thrombo-Embolic Disease) stockings should be worn.

16. I

The anti-phospholipid antibody (Hughes') syndrome may occur on its own or in association with other connective tissue diseases, especially lupus. It is characterised by a history of recurrent arterial and/or venous thrombosis, migraine, miscarriages and thrombocytopenia. Livedo reticularis is often seen on the legs. Aspirin reduces the risk of further miscarriage and life-long high-dose warfarin should be prescribed after any major thrombotic event.

17. K

A severe pulmonary embolism affecting a central pulmonary artery is an indication for thrombolysis or, even, embolectomy. This may be life saving and should not be delayed for definitive imaging to be performed.

Theme: Planning and management of patients with head injury

18. C

A trivial head injury with no loss of consciousness and no neurological symptoms or signs does not require admission even if there is nobody at the patient's home. He must be advised to return to casualty if he feels drowsy, vomits or develops neurological symptoms. He should also be advised to ask someone to check on him in a few hours' time.

19. I

Head injury with loss of consciousness and amnesia requires a skull X-ray. X-ray is also indicated in the presence of CSF rhinorrhoea or otorrhoea; neurological symptoms or signs; significant external head injury; or where assessment is difficult (i.e. the extremes of age or intoxication). The presence of a skull fracture increases the risk of intracranial haemorrhage from <1/1000 to 1/30, in an alert patient; and from 1/100 to 1/4, in a confused patient. In this case, if the skull X-ray is normal, the patient may be discharged home with advice. Admission for observation is probably a safer option, unless the loss of consciousness was truly brief.

20. D

Base-of-skull fracture may cause CSF rhinorrhoea or otorrhoea and bilateral peri-orbital haematomata. If there is doubt whether the nasal fluid is CSF, it should be tested with a glucose-testing strip. CSF contains glucose; mucus does not. Base-of-skull fracture is treated as an open fracture with antibiotics. CT brain should be performed, as the diagnosis may be missed on plain X-rays.

21. A

All children should be admitted after a significant head injury. In this case, even if the head injury was trivial, the child should be admitted. The presence of multiple bruises, which do not sound consistent with the mechanism of injury, raises the possibility of non-accidental injury.

22. E

Unfortunately, this scenario may still, occasionally, occur in peripheral hospitals. The clinical scenario is very suggestive of raised intracranial pressure secondary to an extradural haematoma. Clearly there is not time to arrange diagnostic investigations or definitive treatment. A burr hole might be life saving if the diagnosis is correct. It is unlikely to do harm if the diagnosis is wrong. Usually, but not always, the haematoma is ipsilateral to the dilated pupil. If the initial burr hole does not produce results and the patient is deteriorating, then a contralateral burr hole may also be tried. It is not unusual for both pupils to be dilated, in which case bilateral burr holes are usually required if a CT scan is unavailable.

23. I

Skull X-rays should be performed, in the first instance, for three reasons: He has a significant scalp laceration, he has been drinking and he may have been assaulted (so the X-rays may be useful from a forensic point of view). He should be admitted overnight, as he will be unobserved if he is discharged. There is a higher incidence of extradural and subdural haemorrhage in alcoholics. Misdiagnosis is common due to difficulties in assessing patients who are confused or inebriated. You should have a low threshold for arranging a CT scan.

Theme: Prescribing for patients in renal failure

The kidneys eliminate many drugs or their metabolites. If renal clearance is reduced, the drug or metabolite may be retained and reach toxic levels. Different drugs are affected in different ways. Less commonly, reduced renal function requires a higher dose of the drug for it to be effective. This particularly applies to drugs that act upon the nephron.

24. B

Captopril may become toxic if creatinine clearance is low. The risk of cardiovascular side-effects is greater. It is recommended that the starting dose is reduced and that the patient's renal function is monitored more regularly. ACE inhibitors are contraindicated in patients with bilateral renal artery stenosis or unilateral renal artery stenosis supplying a single functioning kidney. In these situations, reduction in angiotensin II may lead to rapid deterioration in renal function. Particular care should be taken in prescribing NSAIDs in combination with ACE inhibitors. Creatinine clearance in patients with renal artery stenosis may be well preserved and serum creatinine may be normal. ACE inhibitors are being used increasingly by renal specialists for controlling hypertension in patients with renal disease with good evidence of a protective effect.

25. G

Gentamicin excretion is very sensitive to reduction in renal function. It is also nephrotoxic, especially when given in combination with loop diuretics. Patients should have Gentamicin levels monitored routinely. In renal impairment, monitoring should be more frequent and the dose will probably be lower. Loading dose remains the same but the dose and/or the frequency may need adjusting. It is standard practice to measure peak (post-dose) and trough (pre-dose) levels. If the peak levels are high, the dose needs reducing. If the trough levels are high, the frequency needs reducing.

26. **F**

Frusemide acts on the loop of Henlé in the nephron. Consequently, if the number of functioning nephrons are reduced, the dose of frusemide may need increasing accordingly to achieve the same diuretic effect. It is not uncommon for patients in acute renal failure to be given 250 mg of frusemide over one hour in an attempt to mount a diuresis. It is important to monitor renal function as it may deteriorate with the administration of any diuretic. Higher doses must be given slowly to reduce the risk of drug-induced deafness.

27. **A**

Phenytoin is metabolised by the liver and is largely protein-bound in the blood. It is unaffected by renal function but may be affected by liver disease or by co-administration of drugs that are also protein-bound. Theoretically, in nephrotic syndrome, hypoproteinaemia may affect phenytoin levels.

28. **C**

Most cephalosporins are excreted unchanged by the kidney and will accumulate in renal failure. Even in mild renal failure, some dose adjustment is required. In most cases, this means a reduction in dose frequency (bd instead of tds in mild or moderate renal impairment, od in severe renal impairment). It is often forgotten that renal function in older patients may be impaired even in the presence of a relatively normal creatinine. A 75-year-old of normal body weight with a creatinine of 100 mmol/l will have at least mildly impaired creatinine clearance.

Theme: Investigation of urinary tract symptoms

29. **D**

Pyelonephritis is common in young women and the organism is usually a coliform. Failure to respond promptly to antibiotics raises the possibility of an obstructed infected kidney, a pyonephrosis. Renal ultrasound will show evidence of obstruction and dilatation of the renal pelvis and calyces. IVU will also make the diagnosis but there is a small risk of precipitating renal failure secondary to contrast nephropathy. If the infection is walled-off in an obstructed kidney, treatment is with urgent nephrostomy, which may also be carried out under ultrasound.

30. **L**

Urethritis is usually due to a sexually transmitted organism such as gonococcus or chlamydia. It may be suspected by a positive three-glass test: urine is collected in three consecutive beakers – cloudy urine in the first glass, clear in the third) and diagnosed with microscopy and culture of a urethral swab. Special culture media are required.

31. **J**

New urinary symptoms should always warrant at least one random blood glucose measurement. The diagnosis of diabetes may be made with a single fasting glucose >7 mmol/l (or a random glucose > 11.1 mmol/l) in a patient with symptoms of hyperglycaemia (thirst, polyuria, weight loss, blurred vision or ketoacidosis).

32. **G**

Painless haematuria is the commonest presenting symptom of bladder carcinoma. It may also be caused by cystitis, bladder diverticulae or prostatic hypertrophy. All of these diagnoses may be made by cystoscopy and biopsies may be taken at the same time. Rubber workers are at increased risk due to contact with aromatic amines.

33. H

Pneumaturia (passing bubbles in the urine) is a symptom of fistulae between the bladder and colon or rectum. It may also occur in urinary infections due to gas-forming organisms, which sometimes occurs in patients with diabetes. A large fistula may also result in faecal matter being passed in the urine. Urine culture will show a heavy mixed growth of bowel flora. Pelvic malignancy and radiotherapy are rare causes. Fistulae are usually secondary to diverticular disease, Crohn's disease, trauma or carcinoma of the colon or bladder. Investigation is barium enema, looking for extra-luminal barium and identification of the underlying cause.

Theme: Investigation of acute abdominal pain

34.   J

She has peritonism and shock. This may be due to a perforated viscus (e.g. appendix or peptic ulcer) or rupture of an ovarian cyst or ectopic pregnancy (the most likely diagnosis). She is acutely unwell and will require an urgent laparotomy regardless of the cause. A positive β HCG must be performed first. This will identify an ectopic pregnancy, in which case the surgery should be performed by a gynaecologist and a greater amount of blood loss should be expected.

35.   E

This patient has peritonitis that has presented early, before the development of systemic compromise. The history suggests that the underlying cause is a perforated peptic ulcer. Erect chest X-ray will show air under the diaphragm and a laparotomy should be performed promptly. If the patient is too unwell to sit up, the diagnosis of perforation may also be made with a lateral decubitus abdominal X-ray. If an X-ray is not forthcoming, a diagnostic aspirate of the peritoneal cavity may be made, cautiously, with a 14 gauge needle. If the aspirate appears faecal or haemorrhagic, the diagnosis is probably perforation (rarely spontaneous bacterial peritonitis or necrotic pancreatitis).

36.   A

A very high amylase has high sensitivity for diagnosing acute pancreatitis, except in a patient with underlying severe chronic pancreatitis. The combination of severe abdominal symptoms and milder abdominal signs is suggestive of acute pancreatitis. Abdominal ultrasound or CT will confirm the diagnosis and identify gallstones, if present.

37. G

Lower chest injuries may be associated with rupture of liver or spleen. Splenic rupture may present immediately or after a delay of hours, even days. The signs are peritonism and shock that is out of proportion to the degree of observed blood loss or apparent trauma. The patient may be tender locally, in the left upper quadrant, or generally. Ultrasound or CT scan will show the splenic rupture but if the patient is shocked and there is likely to be any delay in arranging imaging (e.g. outside of working hours), diagnostic peritoneal lavage will confirm the presence of intra-peritoneal haemorrhage. Laparotomy need not wait for imaging.

38. F

Bowel obstruction is diagnosed by plain abdominal X-ray. Traditionally, both an erect and a supine film are requested. The supine film would show dilated loops of bowel and the erect film would show multiple fluid levels in the dilated, obstructed bowel. There is little evidence that a second film increases the diagnostic sensitivity and only a supine film is requested routinely. This patient's obstruction is secondary to an obstructed, strangulated femoral hernia, the diagnosis of which is clinical.

39. L

If this patient were well enough, ultrasound or CT of his abdomen would confirm the diagnosis of a ruptured abdominal aortic aneurysm. However, he is too unstable to delay surgery a moment longer than necessary. Any delay increases the risk of intra-operative death or post-operative renal failure. Shock should be treated with aggressive fluid resuscitation and transfusion, aiming for a systolic BP of 100 mmHg (but no higher). You do not have time to wait for cross-matched blood (though he will need at least 10 units of cross-matched blood during the operation) so he should be given O –ve until cross-matched blood is available.

Theme: Symptoms and signs of normal pregnancy

40. A

Morning sickness is very common and usually occurs between the 4th and 14th weeks of pregnancy. It is largely caused by circulating β HCG. It is usually managed with frequent small low-calorie meals. Occasionally cyclizine is used as an anti-emetic. Severe sickness, hyperemesis gravidarum, occurs in about 1/1000 pregnancies. Mothers may be unable to keep any food or fluids down with resultant weight loss and dehydration. In-patient treatment with anti-emetics and intravenous fluids is often required. In severe vomiting, causes of an abnormally high β HCG (twins, trophoblastic disease) should be excluded with a pelvic ultrasound.

41. D

First fetal movements ('quickening') are usually felt at around 20 weeks in a primigravida mother and 16–18 weeks in subsequent pregnancies.

42. G

Low back pain is caused by relaxation of pelvic muscles and ligaments towards the end of pregnancy. The pain is typically worse at night. Improved posture, flat shoes and a firm mattress may alleviate it. Back pain is often more severe if the fetus is lying posteriorly.

43. C

Breast and nipple enlargement occurs in the first few weeks in response to high levels of oestrogen and human placental lactogen. HPL also stimulates production of growth hormone and insulin. Excess growth hormone, in turn, produces thyroid enlargement and increased thyroxine production. Nipple and areolar darkening occurs around 12 weeks due to increased vascularity and the effect of increased melanocyte stimulating hormone. Pigmented naevi often darken and pigmented patches on the cheeks (melasma or chloasma) also appear.

44. I

Pregnancy causes a gradual increase in red cell production by around 30%. It also causes more rapid plasma volume expansion by over 50%. This results in relative haemodilution, despite an absolute increase in red cell mass, and a drop in haemoglobin concentration and haematocrit.

Theme: Immediate investigation of unconscious patient

45. G

This patient has a picture consistent with raised intracranial pressure secondary to a subarachnoid haemorrhage. Lumbar puncture is more sensitive than CT head for diagnosing subarachnoid haemorrhage. In an uncomplicated subarachnoid haemorrhage, CT brain may be normal in up to 20% of cases. Nonetheless, in this instance a CT scan must be performed first in order to confirm or exclude the presence of raised intracranial pressure. If so, lumbar puncture is contraindicated and, more importantly, this would be an indication for urgent neurosurgery to treat any developing hydrocephalus.

46. D

This suggests a myocardial infarction complicated by an arrhythmia. The temptation is to defibrillate immediately but this may do more harm without first identifying the rhythm. Ventricular tachycardia or fibrillation should be treated with DC shock. Supraventricular arrhythmias, however, must receive a synchronised shock so as to avoid delivering the electrical impulse at the same time as the T wave, which might convert the SVT to VT or VF. It is also possible that the patient has a bradyarrhythmia, which might require atropine, isoprenaline or pacing. Alternatively the rate and rhythm might be normal and the collapse due to ventricular rupture, tamponade or acute mitral regurgitation.

47. A

Hypoglycaemia is often precipitated in people with diabetes by drinking alcohol. Many neglect to eat but still take their usual dose of insulin. Confusion is often rapidly followed by coma and/or convulsions. Patients are advised to carry a card or bracelet to identify them as having diabetes, but many prefer to avoid being labelled as having a disease.

48.   K

A pneumothorax is more common and more serious in patients with chronic lung disease than in normal individuals. A small pneumothorax may be easily missed clinically in an asthmatic, as the movement of air may be generally poor. A tension pneumothorax is diagnosed clinically with evidence of cardiac compromise and mediastinal shift. If suspected, you should proceed to treat without waiting for a chest X-ray, as any delay may be fatal. Firstly insert a large cannula in the second intercostal space on the affected side (you should hear a rapid escape of air) before proceeding to insert a chest drain. In the unlikely event of an incorrect diagnosis, the cannula will do no harm. It is said that, ideally, no X-ray of a tension pneumothorax should exist; though many do.

49.   A

Hypoglycaemia is common and, unless thought of, may be missed. I make no apologies for including this diagnosis in more than one question, as it is a favourite of examiners. Hyperglycaemia rarely causes fits except as part of a hyperosmolar non-ketotic state in older patients. Hypoglycaemia should always be excluded by checking a formal laboratory blood glucose. Capillary blood glucose readings may be falsely elevated if the skin is inadequately cleaned; and may be falsely low if too small a drop of blood is used. The reading of 18 mmol/l is probably spurious or misleading and should be repeated in any event.

Theme: Interpretation of haematological results

50. C

Anaemia with a low-normal MCV suggests either partially treated iron deficiency, mixed haematinic deficiency, thalassaemia or anaemia of chronic disease. A high ferritin excludes the first two possibilities. In a 40-year-old woman, chronic disease is the most likely cause and rheumatoid arthritis is a common chronic disease that causes anaemia. A moderately elevated platelet count is also consistent with an inflammatory condition.

51. G

Macrocytosis, anaemia and neutropenia suggest megaloblastic anaemia, which is caused by deficiency of vitamin B12 or folate. Phenytoin impairs folate metabolism and causes actual or functional folate deficiency. Macrocytosis, without anaemia, is very common in patients treated with phenytoin.

52. A

Minor thalassaemias (β or α) cause mild anaemia with microcytosis out of proportion to the mean cell haemoglobin. They also cause an elevated red cell count, which helps to distinguish them from iron deficiency. HbA_2 is formed by 2 α chains and 2 δ chains and is found in low levels ($<3\%$) in normal individuals. Levels are increased where β chain production is impaired. The anaemia is rarely of clinical significance except in pregnancy.

53. E

Myeloblasts are seen in myeloid leukaemia, leukaemoid reaction, leukoerythroblastic syndromes and myelodysplasia. Myelodysplasia is common in the elderly but is not a feature of normal ageing. Any or all of the cell lines may be reduced. Monocytosis and mild macrocytosis is common and small numbers of myeloblasts may occur. There is no specific treatment, although folate supplements may help. Treatment is symptomatic – transfusion for anaemia, antibiotics for infection, platelet transfusions rarely. The condition may transform into acute myeloid leukaemia.

54. **K**

Chronic lymphocytic leukaemia is very common and is often identified as an incidental finding on blood tests in older people. It may also present with lymphadenopathy, hepatosplenomegaly, bruising, anaemia or recurrent infections. There may be associated thrombocytopenia, anaemia, neutropenia or immunoparesis due to marrow infiltration. Anaemia may also occur due to an associated autoimmune haemolytic anaemia, giving a positive direct antiglobulin (Coombs') test, which may be treated with steroids. Occasionally anti-platelet antibodies also occur.

55. **D**

Hypersegmented neutrophils occur in megaloblastic anaemia, uraemia and liver disease. Macrocytosis occurs in megaloblastic anaemia, liver disease, hypothyroidism, myelodysplasia, marrow infiltration, alcohol, pregnancy or haemolysis. Target cells occur in iron deficiency, haemolysis, haemoglobinopathies and liver disease. The common link is liver disease. Alcohol is also directly toxic to platelets.

Theme: Over-the-counter medications

56. H

Thrush may be treated with clotrimazole cream or pessary. Other topical anti-fungal imidazoles are also available over the counter. Oral fluconazole is also available without prescription. Topical clotrimazole is cheaper over the counter than a standard prescription charge.

57. K

Upper gastro-intestinal symptoms in a young man are usually due to benign pathology. Initial advice should be to use proprietary antacids, which usually contain magnesium or aluminium salts, to lose weight, reduce alcohol intake and stop smoking. If the symptoms persist then a diagnostic endoscopy is probably worthwhile in order to look for evidence of peptic ulcer disease and associated *Helicobacter* infection. H_2 antagonists have been available without prescription for a couple of years but are expensive and should not be used first-line.

58. A

The diagnosis is a viral illness, possibly chickenpox. There is no specific treatment indicated for uncomplicated chickenpox. The most important treatment is to reduce her temperature to reduce the risk of a second febrile convulsion. Parents are advised to keep the child in a cool room with minimal clothing, to sponge the child with tepid water and to use a fan. Paracetamol is also useful as an anti-pyretic as well as an analgesic. Aspirin is not recommended because of the risk of Reye's syndrome. If itch is a major problem, topical calamine lotion or an oral antihistamine may be used. Several antihistamines are licensed for use in children, including loratadine, promethazine and chlorpheniramine, but are licensed for allergic conditions and not pruritus. Only one antihistamine, azatadine, is licensed for use in pruritus.

59. F

Several antihistamines are licensed for use in seasonal or perennial allergic rhinitis. Loratadine is a non-sedating antihistamine. Chlorpheniramine is sedating and should be avoided if a patient needs to maintain concentration. An alternative would be for the student to use topical sodium cromoglycate. However a nasal spray alone will not be sufficient, as allergic conjunctivitis is likely to be equally problematic.

60. M

Epigastric pain of recent onset in a middle-aged (or older) patient requires medical assessment to identify those who are at risk of gastric carcinoma. There should be a low threshold for diagnostic endoscopy. Malignant gastric ulcers may respond symptomatically to acid suppression. There was some concern, when H_2 antagonists became widely available, that this would result in delayed presentations of gastric malignancy. There is no evidence that this has actually happened.

Theme: Headache – selection of diagnostic tests

61. **D**

Temporal arteritis should be suspected in any unilateral or severe headache, or in sudden visual loss, in a patient over the age of 50. Symptoms of polymyalgia rheumatica (proximal muscle pain and stiffness) may or may not also be present. Inflammatory markers (ESR, CRP, WCC) are often elevated. If the clinical suspicion is high but the blood tests are normal it is quite reasonable to arrange whether a temporal artery biopsy or a therapeutic trial of high-dose prednisolone. Temporal artery biopsy may also be negative, as the disease is often patchy. The ESR is the investigation of choice, as a patient may be diagnosed and treated on the basis of a classical clinical picture and a raised ESR, but a biopsy is rarely performed without an ESR first. Prednisolone should be started without waiting for the biopsy result.

62. **I**

Migraine commonly presents for the first time in young women and rarely after the age of 40 years. It is often precipitated by oestrogens and is a relative contraindication to the combined oral contraceptive. Migraine attacks are often linked to the menstrual cycle, occurring pre-menstrually or at the beginning of a period. The diagnosis is clinical. Any investigations are only to exclude other conditions if there are atypical features.

63. **G**

Acute sinusitis is usually obvious clinically but may be confirmed with an X-ray of the sinuses, which will show the presence of a fluid level or loss of the usual air space. Rarely, sinusitis may be complicated by meningitis, cerebral abscess, osteomyelitis or orbital cellulitis and should be managed accordingly.

64. H

There is a low likelihood that this patient has a significant head injury in view of the lack of amnesia or unconsciousness. It is not uncommon for patients to develop a delayed post-head injury syndrome with headache, nausea and poor concentration. A skull X-ray is performed to reassure the patient and for medico-legal reasons. A work-related injury or an assault often requires assessment that is not strictly necessary on clinical grounds alone.

65. A

Headache of chronic raised intracranial pressure is often postural, worse in the morning and insidious in onset. A chronic daily headache alone is rarely due to significant pathology but, if there are any other symptoms or signs (e.g. difficulty writing), a CT or MRI scan should be arranged. CT is more readily available than MRI and is equally good at diagnosing space-occupying lesions.

66. C

A sub-acute history of headache with photophobia and mild meningism is usually due to viral illness with or without meningitis. However, bacterial meningitis cannot be excluded on clinical grounds alone and CSF microscopy and culture is required. Many units now have a policy of performing CT brain before any lumbar puncture but this is not necessary in a patient who has no neurological signs.

Theme: Prescribing for pain relief

67. A

Simple analgesia, paracetamol and aspirin, are appropriate for most mild pain. Paracetamol, aspirin and ibuprofen are all licensed for use in children and available over the counter. Due to its anti-platelet action, aspirin is probably not the best choice after dental extraction due to the risk of increased bleeding.

68. G

Simple analgesia is unlikely to be effective in malignant bone pain. If they are ineffective, you could proceed up the 'analgesic ladder' to moderately strong analgesics such as codeine and tramadol. However, bone pain is likely to require strong analgesia and morphine, or similar, should be given. NSAIDs are also useful in managing bone pain and may be given in combination with opiates, reducing the opiate requirement.

69. J

Pain from an acute abdomen requires opiate analgesia. Morphine is contraindicated if acute pancreatitis is suspected, as it can cause spasm of the pancreatic duct. Pethidine is of similar analgesic potency but without this adverse effect.

70. E

Acute gout may be precipitated by loop diuretics. Pain is due to an intense localised inflammatory process and is best treated with anti-inflammatory drugs. Ibuprofen in high dose may be effective but diclofenac is more potent and probably the drug of first choice. If a patient is unable to take NSAIDs then colchicine or prednisolone are reasonable alternatives.

71. K

Neuropathic pain following herpes zoster, or due to trigeminal neuralgia, amputation or peripheral neuropathy, is difficult to treat with conventional analgesics. Co-analgesics may be of greater benefit. Carbamazepine is of particular use in post-herpetic neuralgia. Other anticonvulsants such as gabapentin, sodium valproate and phenytoin may also be effective. Other classes of co-analgesics include low-dose tricyclic anti-depressants and local anaesthetic-like drugs (e.g. mexiletine). Occasionally the pain remains resistant to treatment and so severe that ganglion ablation is tried.

72. **I**

Many acute procedural pains may be managed with inhaled nitrous oxide mixed with oxygen. This may be used for minor orthopaedic procedures, such as reduction of a finger dislocation. It may also be used in labour and in the management of painful sickle cell crises. Obviously the patient with the finger dislocation could also receive a local anaesthetic ring block.

Theme: Management of diabetes mellitus

73. **D**

This patient will almost certainly have type 2 diabetes. Diet alone will control many of these patients. If not, the patient requires an oral hypoglycaemic agent. Biguanides (metformin) are the drug of choice if the patient is obese unless they have cardiac or renal failure. Sulphonylureas are the drugs of choice if the patient is not obese. In older patients, a short-acting agent minimises the risk of hypoglycaemia or drug accumulation if there is impairment of renal function. Glibenclamide and chlorpropamide are longest acting and, therefore, least safe. Gliclazide and tolbutamide are shorter-acting and safer.

74. **F**

Gestational diabetes (diabetes arising for the first time in pregnancy) is often treatable with diet alone. The patient requires good education and must be encouraged to monitor blood glucose at home. A minority will require insulin to achieve glycaemic control. Oral hypoglycaemics should not be used in pregnancy. Glycosuria is common in pregnancy due to lowering of the renal threshold. If glycosuria is persistently present, a glucose tolerance test should be performed. Some women with gestational diabetes either remain diabetic or subsequently develop diabetes.

75. **J**

There is good evidence that cardiac mortality is reduced with the use of insulin following myocardial infarction. Any patient with a known diagnosis of diabetes, regardless of treatment, or with a glucose greater than 8.0 mmol/l at presentation with an acute MI, should receive insulin therapy. The regime used in the landmark trial was three days on an intravenous insulin sliding scale followed by three months subcutaneous insulin. The sub-group of patients converted to insulin from sulphonylureas benefited the most.

76. **A**

This man's type 2 diabetes is inadequately controlled (pre-meal blood glucose should be 4–7 mmol/l and HbA1c should be < 7.0%). Metformin is the drug of choice, as he is obese. If this fails, acarbose or a sulphonylurea may be tried.

77. **I**

Pregnant women with diabetes have an increased risk of most maternal and fetal complications, and an increased risk of accelerated complication of diabetes. Particular risks are intra-uterine death, premature labour, pre-eclampsia, congenital malformations and neonatal mortality. There is good evidence that tight glycaemic control improves outcome but at the expense of increasing the mother's risk of hypoglycaemia. A qds regime (three injections of soluble insulin and one injection of long-acting insulin) has recently been shown to reduce the risk of hypos. The patient in this question will require considerable support and education.

78. **G**

A patient with type 2 diabetes may require insulin if good glycaemic control cannot be achieved with diet and oral medication. If a patient is on metformin and a sulphonylurea and is obese then acarbose, repaglinide or rosiglitazone may be tried. If they are not obese, insulin is required. Insulin may be given instead of oral medication. It is more usual to add a once daily dose of long-acting insulin to the oral regime. This patient is symptomatic so should probably receive insulin even if he is obese.

Theme: Causes of vaginal bleeding

79. I

The most common cause for any period of amenorrhoea in a sexually active woman of childbearing age is pregnancy. A large number of pregnancies (estimates range from 20–75%) spontaneously abort in the first trimester, often before the pregnancy has declared itself. An unusually heavy period may represent the passage of early fetal and placental material and fetal parts may not be recognised as such. If the patient was unwell or had ongoing bleeding, she should have an ultrasound and uterine curettage to exclude and treat retained products.

80. D

The cervical canal is lined with columnar epithelium (which appears red) and the visible part of the cervix is lined with squamous epithelium (pink). The oral contraceptive increases the columnar zone such that it is visible around the cervical os, which is termed cervical ectropion. Columnar epithelium is more friable and tends to bleed or produce mucus. It is also more prone to infection. Another, misleading, name for this condition is cervical erosion. If there is any doubt about the diagnosis, cervical swab and smear should be performed, looking for infection and neoplasia.

81. K

Post-menopausal bleeding should be assumed to be due to endometrial carcinoma until proven otherwise. Other causes include polyps, vaginitis and foreign bodies. Prolapse on its own rarely causes bleeding unless there is cervical erosion or infection. Normal uterine curettage excludes a diagnosis of endometrial carcinoma. The most likely diagnosis is vaginal or cervical erosion due to a ring pessary that has not been changed.

82. H

Pelvic inflammatory disease increases the risk of ectopic pregnancy due to blockage of one or both Fallopian tubes. The pain of a non-ruptured ectopic is due to tubal colic and often precedes the vaginal bleeding as the uterine lining is shed. Bleeding is typically dark (like prune juice). The history of irregular periods may have masked the amenorrhoea of pregnancy.

83. E

Atrophic vaginitis and vaginal dryness is common in post-menopausal women due to oestrogen deficiency. It may present with vaginal bleeding, dyspareunia, urinary infection, stress incontinence or prolapse. Topical or systemic oestrogen replacement is often of symptomatic benefit.

Theme: Management of drug dependency

84. E

A large number of older patients take benzodiazepines regularly, particularly temazepam and nitrazepam. Withdrawal symptoms are very common if the drug has been taken regularly for longer than six months. There is good evidence in published trials that sedative medications increase the risk of falls and that sedative withdrawal reduces this risk. Withdrawal is easier from longer-acting benzodiazepines, such as diazepam or chlordiazepoxide. The patient should be converted to an equivalent dose of diazepam, which is then reduced by 2 mg every one or two weeks. Many patients are unable or unwilling to discontinue these drugs.

85. C

Obviously you will try hard to encourage this patient to consider a drug withdrawal programme or a methadone maintenance programme. In this case, your priority is to reduce her risk of needle-related infections (HIV, hepatitis B and C) and advise a needle exchange programme. Although abuse of drugs is a criminal offence, patient confidentiality does not allow you to inform the police. It is a duty, however, to make sure that she is registered as a drug addict. The Regional Health Authority holds a confidential register.

86. J

Alcohol dependence is often precipitated by bereavement, in the false belief that it alleviates the symptoms of depression. In fact, alcohol is a depressant and will exacerbate the problem. Treatment is only beneficial if the patient recognises the problem and wants to give up drinking. Even so, the relapse rate is high. Supportive counselling and group psychotherapy (e.g. Alcoholics Anonymous) is of most benefit. Disulfiram may be used in patients experiencing difficulty abstaining. It produces an unpleasant reaction (flushing and nausea) when taken with alcohol, which discourages a patient from drinking.

87. **E**

Alcohol withdrawal (delirium tremens) is unpredictable and does not occur in all patients who abstain after drinking heavily. It presents between one and three days after the last drink and is a common occurrence on surgical wards amongst post-operative patients. There are differing schools of thought regarding alcohol withdrawal. Some favour routine use of benzodiazepines for all patients, believing this to be safest and kindest to patients. Others adopt a wait-and-see policy for most patients, in the belief that to prescribe benzodiazepines is merely exchanging one addiction for another with the potential for causing greater harm. A pragmatic approach is to use prophylaxis for very heavy drinkers, patients with a history of withdrawal seizures or delirium tremens and patients in whom an episode of delirium may impair recovery (e.g. following orthopaedic surgery). Chlormethiazole is rarely used now because the risk of respiratory depression is greater than with other benzodiazepines.

88. **D**

Confusion, ataxia, nystagmus and ophthalmoplegia are features of Wernicke's encephalopathy. Dementia, impairment of new learning, confabulation and paranoia are features of Korsakoff's psychosis. Both syndromes are caused by thiamine deficiency, usually secondary to alcohol abuse. Acute symptoms often respond to parenteral thiamine. Chronic symptoms rarely improve. It is important not to assume that paranoid symptoms are delusional, as occasionally they may turn out to be well founded!

89. **F**

If a drug addict has adequate social support, there is no reason why they should require in-patient treatment. Drug dependency teams can arrange supported outpatient withdrawal programmes.

Theme: Advice for travellers – vaccinations

Any traveller intending to visit a high-risk area should seek expert advice. Vaccination alone is not enough and travellers should also be advised to use insect nets and sprays and to avoid insect and animal bites. They should also be advised to take condoms (and use them).

90. I

Sub-Saharan Africa has a high level of endemic infections and a broad vaccination programme is recommended. Many countries, but not Somalia, insist upon written proof of yellow fever vaccination.

91. G

South East Asia is another high-risk area. Sexually transmitted diseases are common and, apart from hepatitis B, there are no vaccines available as yet.

92. D

Travellers to the Caribbean are advised to have hepatitis A, typhoid and polio vaccinations. Childhood polio vaccination does not offer lifelong protection; adults are advised to be revaccinated at the same time as their children. Hepatitis A infection probably gives lifelong immunity and so this patient does not need vaccination against it, although it will do him no harm if there is any doubt.

93. A

Rabies has been eradicated from the United Kingdom but is still present in rural areas of other European countries. The risk is small and rabies vaccine is not given routinely for travel to Western Europe.

Theme: Management of complications of pregnancy

94. D

This is hyperemesis gravidarum, which requires admission to hospital if there is evidence of dehydration. Ketonuria is common after vomiting. Urinary tract infection is unlikely in the absence of nitrites on dipstick. Management is intravenous fluid replacement. Anti-emetics (cyclizine or metoclopramide) may be required.

95. A

Massive antepartum haemorrhage almost always requires urgent resuscitation and delivery. A massive painless bleed is usually due to placenta praevia, in which case vaginal delivery is contraindicated and an emergency Caesarean is required, especially if the fetus is still alive. The patient should receive resuscitation with fluid and blood but the definitive management is delivery to treat the cause of the bleeding.

96. K

Amniotic fluid embolism is a recognised complication of amniocentesis. It presents with sudden cyanosis and collapse, often with shock or seizures. It may be complicated by DIC (disseminated intravascular coagulation). The most important management is to ensure adequate oxygenation. If a facemask does not correct the hypoxia, she will require intubation and ventilation. Any hypotension should be corrected with intravenous fluids. Over-hydration should be avoided as it may lead to adult respiratory distress syndrome (ARDS).

97. L

Mild leg oedema and cramps are common, occurring in about one-third of normal pregnancies. Symptomatic DVT will usually present as a unilateral, tense, tender, warm leg. This patient can be reassured and given advice about what symptoms and signs to look out for.

98. J

Pre-eclampsia is more common in first pregnancy and mothers at the extremes of age. Hypertension and proteinuria are the principal features. Mothers should be admitted if they are symptomatic (nausea, headache, fever, vomiting, epigastric or chest pain, tremor). Admission is also advisable if BP has risen > 30/20 more than their booking BP, if it is ≥ 160/100, or ≥ 140/90 with proteinuria. Symptomatic pre-eclampsia or rising blood pressure requires treatment with methyldopa, hydralazine or labetalol. Timing of delivery requires expert opinion and is guided by increasing symptoms, fetal distress or lack of response to treatment.

99. A

Placental abruption tends to cause shock that is out of proportion to the amount of visible blood loss. Urgent resuscitation and delivery is required in the presence of shock or fetal distress (a low fetal heart rate is more serious than a high rate). In milder cases, induction of labour may be considered if placenta praevia is excluded on ultrasound. If the fetus has died and the mother is stable, emergency section is also unnecessary.

Theme: Prescribing in pregnancy

100. A

ACE inhibitors are contraindicated in all trimesters of pregnancy. They cross the placenta and affect organogenesis and growth. They are associated with renal agenesis, renal impairment, oligohydramnios and skull defects. There is good evidence that progression of diabetic nephropathy may be reduced with anti-hypertensive agents other than ACE inhibitors.

101. F

Warfarin causes congenital malformations if given during the first trimester and fetal or neonatal haemorrhage if given prior to delivery. Conradi-Hünermann syndrome is the name given to the syndrome that occurs with warfarin use in the first trimester. Clinical features include saddle nose, frontal bossing, short stature, epiphyseal stippling (on X-ray), optic atrophy, cataracts and learning difficulties. Warfarin is relatively safe in the second trimester, although some physicians favour the use of heparin throughout pregnancy. The management of patients with mechanical heart valves is more controversial and needs specialist care.

Heparin increases the risk of ante- and peri-partum haemorrhage. It is also associated with osteoporosis with prolonged usage. It may be used cautiously in pregnancy except immediately before delivery. It is used in preference to warfarin in the first and third trimesters. Most low molecular weight heparins do not yet have a license for use in pregnancy but are prescribed by some specialists.

102. H

Carbamazepine, phenytoin and sodium valproate are all associated with teratogenesis, particularly neural tube defects. These are more common with valproate. However, the risk to mother and fetus due to uncontrolled epilepsy is greater than the risk due to the medication. In an ideal situation, pre-conception counselling by a specialist may identify patients who may change or be withdrawn from their medication. Risk of neural tube defects may be reduced by folate supplementation. Carbamazepine and phenytoin also increased the risk of haemorrhagic disease of the newborn, so both mother and baby should receive vitamin K. Lamotrigine may be safer than traditional agents.

103. B

Trimethoprim is a folate antagonist and, therefore, has theoretical risks of neural tube defects if given in the first trimester. Penicillins and cephalosporins are not known to be harmful. Sulphonamides may cause haemolysis if given in the third trimester. Tetracycline may cause skeletal abnormalities (first trimester) or dental discoloration (second and third trimesters).

104. A

Glibenclamide only causes fetal problems when given late in the third trimester, when it may induce fetal hypoglycaemia and convulsions. However, the risk of complications of pregnancy in women with diabetes is lower when managed with insulin. Ideally, women with diabetes should be treated with a qds insulin regimen as this reduces the risk of hypoglycaemia compared to a bd regimen. Metformin is contraindicated in all trimesters of pregnancy.

Theme: Causes of respiratory symptoms in children

105. E

Whooping cough (pertussis) is rare in the UK thanks to an effective vaccination programme. Pertussis vaccination is very rarely (< 1/100,000) associated with severe brain injury and may cause epilepsy. Uptake of the vaccine is not 100% due to parental fears about vaccine safety after high-profile publicity of adverse neurological effects. The disease is often chronic and misdiagnosed as asthma or pneumonia. Absence of significant wheeze or fever and presence of a lymphocytosis are suggestive. Complications include neurological damage, bronchiectasis and death. Treatment with erythromycin is of unproved benefit.

106. I

Cough with wheeze is most often due to asthma. Localised, monophonic (single-pitched) wheeze suggests obstruction of a single airway. A common cause in young children is inhalation of a foreign body, often without any history to confirm this. Inhaled foreign objects are most likely to become trapped in the bronchus to the right lower lobe. A chest X-ray often makes the diagnosis. Otherwise diagnosis and treatment is with bronchoscopy.

107. G

Diphtheria has almost been eradicated from the United Kingdom. Political turmoil and increasing poverty in Eastern Europe and the former Soviet states have caused a massive increase in the number of cases of diphtheria. It is highly infectious so early identification and contact tracing is important. Diagnosis should be suspected clinically by the presence of a fever and adherent membrane over the tonsils, palate or uvula. Tachycardia, out of proportion to the degree of fever, suggests myocarditis, which may be irreversible or fatal. Diagnose with culture of a throat swab. Treat early with diphtheria antitoxin and penicillin or erythromycin.

108. B

Nasal flaring, grunting, intercostal recession, increased respiratory effort and cyanosis are signs of respiratory distress in children and require urgent attention. In a child of this age, the most common cause of respiratory distress is acute bronchiolitis. Diagnosis is largely clinical. The causative agent is nearly always respiratory syncytial virus. Treat with humidified oxygen and amoxicillin and flucloxacillin to prevent secondary infection.

109. J

Oesophageal atresia and tracheo-oesophageal fistulae may present immediately after birth with inability to feed. They may also present with failure to thrive, nasal regurgitation, recurrent aspiration pneumonia, cough or cyanosis. Passage of a naso-gastric tube is impossible. Diagnose with endoscopy and treat with surgical repair.

Theme: Causes of pre- and perinatal infections

110. F

Congenital HIV infection is becoming increasingly common in the United Kingdom and is very common worldwide. Mothers are often unaware of their HIV status and are not screened routinely in antenatal clinic. If maternal HIV infection is known and the pregnancy continues, the risk of vertical transmission is reduced with zidovudine and elective Caesarean section. Neonatal diagnosis is difficult because maternal HIV antibodies cross the placenta. You should look for IgM antibodies after about 3–6 months. Congenital infection presents after around six months with failure to thrive, diarrhoea and fevers. Lymphadenopathy, dermatitis, thrush and other opportunistic infections may also occur.

111. E

Congenital toxoplasma and CMV syndromes are similar. Both may cause learning difficulties, hepatosplenomegaly, jaundice, cerebral palsy, growth delay and cataract. CMV is more common and tends to cause retinal disease. 5/1000 births are infected with CMV of whom 5–10% develops handicap. There is no prevention or treatment. Risk of toxoplasma infection may be reduced by the mother avoiding contact with soil, cat faeces and poorly cooked meat.

112. G

Neonatal meningitis is caused by infection with organisms from the birth canal. Organisms include Listeria, *E. coli* and Group B streptococcus, which is the most common. Listeria tends to cause septicaemia and pneumonia in addition to meningitis and may induce premature labour. Diagnosis of meningitis is difficult clinically and all neonates with fever or sepsis should have a full septic screen including lumbar puncture. In addition, it is worth taking a vaginal swab from the mother to look for streptococcus.

113. B

Neonatal herpes infection is usually due to herpes simplex virus type 2. If the mother has active genital herpes there is a 50% risk of transmission to the neonate, which may be reduced by Caesarean delivery before or soon after the membranes rupture. Clinical infection occurs within the first three weeks with a characteristic rash on the presenting part. Other features include lymphadenopathy, hepatosplenomegaly, jaundice, encephalitis and collapse. Treat with aciclovir and isolate the baby.

114. I

Congenital chlamydia infection may cause conjunctivitis with or without pneumonia in the first two weeks after delivery. It is a common cause of visual impairment worldwide but rare in the UK. Diagnose with culture or immunofluorescence. Treat the neonate with topical tetracycline and oral erythromycin. Treat both parents also with oral tetracycline or erythromycin.

Theme: Choice of treatment for arrhythmias

115. D

A short PR interval and delta wave are signs of ventricular pre-excitation due to a fast-conducting accessory pathway. This is Wolff-Parkinson-White syndrome which is associated with both ventricular and supraventricular arrhythmias. Drugs that work exclusively on the atrio-ventricular node (Digoxin) are contraindicated as this might lead to unopposed rapid conduction through the accessory pathway and ventricular tachycardia. A class III drug like amiodarone or sotalol will control SVT or ventricular arrhythmias without this risk. In a young woman, sotalol should be used first, as there is high incidence of side-effects with amiodarone when used long term.

116. G

Short runs of VT are common during thrombolysis and reperfusion after myocardial infarction. If the patient is uncompromised and the runs are short and self-terminating, no treatment is required. If the runs persist and the patient is symptomatic, lignocaine is the drug of choice, even though it is negatively inotropic. If the patient collapses or develops major haemodynamic compromise, he should receive a pre-cordial thump (witnessed and monitored VT or VF only) and emergency cardioversion if that fails.

117. A

Women at risk of SVT are more likely to develop symptoms during pregnancy as a result of increased levels of catecholamines. If the episode is symptomatic and does not self-terminate then treatment is required. Vagal manoeuvres such as carotid sinus massage should be tried first, as this is unlikely to affect the fetus. If this fails there are a number of options, all of which may affect the fetal heart rate and so must be accompanied with maternal and fetal monitoring. Adenosine is very short acting and probably the drug of first choice. Other options are intravenous verapamil or esmolol given cautiously.

118. L

A broad complex tachycardia may be due to VT or SVT with aberrant ventricular conduction. If a patient has collapsed or is shocked there is no time to distinguish between them and they should receive emergency DC cardioversion.

119. H

It is most likely that this man has become hyperkalaemic due to peritonitis as a complication of peritoneal dialysis. Cardiac stabilisation may be achieved with intravenous administration of calcium chloride or calcium gluconate. This may rapidly convert a severely abnormal ECG to a normal one. This is only a temporary measure until the hyperkalaemia can be corrected with insulin/dextrose infusion or dialysis.

Theme: Management of hyperlipidaemia

These questions and answers are based on the British Hyperlipidaemia Association (BHA) guidelines. Primary hypercholesterolaemia without other modifiable cardiovascular risk factors should be treated with diet in the first instance. The BHA recommends two levels of dietary fat restriction, reserving the step 2 diet (answer F) for patients who have not reached desired cholesterol levels with step 1 diet (answer E). All patients with total cholesterol > 5.2 mmol/l and/or a triglyceride level > 2.3 mmol/l should be advised to follow at least a step 1 diet.

120. C

Undiagnosed or under-treated diabetes causes high lipid levels, particularly triglycerides. Good diet and blood sugar control will often reduce triglycerides to an acceptable level. If diet fails, the treatment of choice for isolated hypertriglyceridaemia is a fibrate. Nicotinic acid is an alternative if fibrates are not tolerated. In mixed hyperlipidaemia, the choice is between a fibrate and atorvastatin.

121. B

There is good evidence that statins prescribed after myocardial infarction reduce cardiovascular mortality. This benefit seems to extend to patients with 'normal' cholesterol levels. A rough target is a level of 4.5 mmol/l or less for total cholesterol. It should also be borne in mind that total cholesterol levels are falsely lowered from about 24 hours to six weeks after a myocardial infarction. A statin is usually prescribed without first attempting a trial of diet.

122. G

Dyslipidaemia is common in patients with primary biliary cirrhosis, who often develop xanthomata and xanthelasma. There is no cure for primary biliary cirrhosis, so the lipids must be corrected actively. Cholestyramine binds bile salts and is used to treat pruritus associated with the disease. It is also reasonably effective in reducing cholesterol but may cause a rise in triglycerides. Dietary restriction should also be advised.

123. I

Excess alcohol may cause dyslipidaemia even in the absence of cirrhosis. Triglycerides are more likely to be raised than cholesterol but both may occur. Cessation of drinking will often reduce both lipids to normal levels without specific treatment. Compliance with abstinence is often poor.

124. E

This patient has established vascular disease, and mixed dyslipidaemia at a moderate level. Dietary advice should be given in the first instance but there should be a low threshold for medical therapy, probably a statin. Many physicians would immediately start a statin.

Theme: Choice of contraception

125. H

The most effective form of contraception is sterilisation of either the male or female partner. If they were quite sure that they do not want further children then this would be the management of choice. Vasectomy is preferable to female sterilisation as it does not require a general anaesthetic and the complication rate is lower. If there is any doubt, an intra-uterine contraceptive device (IUCD) provides good protection with minimal inconvenience. Oestrogen-containing contraception is associated with increased thrombotic complications in older women.

126. E

Oestrogens are relatively contraindicated in women with migraine, preventing the use of the combined oral contraceptive. IUCDs are not recommended in younger women because of the risk of infection and subsequent sub-fertility. Therefore her options are barrier methods, except her partner's latex allergy makes this difficult, or progesterone-only contraception. The progesterone-only pill requires good compliance and must be taken at the same time every day, which makes it less useful for shift workers. The progesterone depot injection is highly effective but rarely used in the UK, although it is popular in the rest of Europe.

127. G

The IUCD is probably the best form of contraception after sterilisation for an older woman in a stable relationship.

128. F

Post-coital contraception aims to prevent implantation in case of fertilisation. One option is high-dose levonorgestrel (either with or without oestradiol) within 72 hours of unprotected intercourse. The other option is insertion of an IUCD within five days. In a young woman, levonorgestrel is the treatment of choice. Vomiting is a common side-effect, particularly if given with oestradiol. The woman should be warned that if she does vomit, she would need to have the tablets represcribed. An anti-emetic is often prescribed in addition (not metoclopramide because of the risk of extrapyramidal side-effects in young women).

129. D

The Catholic faith prohibits the use of contraception of any form. However, this does not mean that a Catholic cannot use contraception if they choose to do so. In this case, the combined pill will provide contraception and regular periods and may also reduce the amount of bleeding and pain.

130. B

Barrier methods will protect her against sexually transmitted viruses (HIV, hepatitis B and C, herpes) as well as pregnancy.

Theme: Interpretation of tests of respiratory disease

131. E

This patient has a respiratory alkalosis caused by hyperventilation. It is relatively acute, as there has been no metabolic compensation. The most likely cause is a panic or anxiety attack. Rare causes are (brain stem) stroke, subarachnoid haemorrhage, meningitis, fever, hyperthyroidism, pregnancy, stimulant drugs and salicylate poisoning.

132. K

Sarcoidosis is more common in young Afro-Caribbean women. It causes pulmonary fibrosis, particularly in the upper lobes, but rarely causes clubbing, unlike fibrosing alveolitis. Lung function tests show a restrictive pattern (low FEV_1 and FVC, high FEV_1/FVC) and reduced transfer factor (a measure of alveolar surface area and gas transfer). Other suggestive features are bilateral hilar lymphadenopathy on chest X-ray, hypercalcaemia and raised serum ACE. Diagnosis is made by demonstrating non-caseating granulomata in a bronchial or lymph node biopsy.

133. A

This patient has obstructive lung function tests with evidence of reversibility. Late-onset asthma is on the increase. A diagnosis of chronic bronchitis would be unlikely in a non-smoker. Prolonged airway inflammation often restricts the response to bronchodilators but will respond to a steroid trial. It is a good idea to perform a steroid trial during a period of stability. If there is no significant improvement in lung function, the patient should not be prescribed steroids for future exacerbations.

134. H

The diagnosis of farmer's lung is rarely this obvious and usually requires some detective work. In acute allergic alveolitis, there is evidence of an inflammatory response with neutrophilia, high ESR and C-reactive protein but little reduction in lung volumes or transfer factor. In chronic alveolitis, inflammatory markers in the blood are normal, chronic inflammatory cells are found in the airways, lung volumes are restricted and transfer factor is reduced. Serum precipitins (tests for allergen-specific IgG) to the causative allergen are positive in both the acute and chronic phases.

135. G

Sudden causes of reduction in lung function are asthma, pneumothorax, pulmonary embolism, pulmonary haemorrhage and removal or collapse of a lobe or lung. Transfer factor (TLCO) measures carbon monoxide uptake and is usually affected only by the loss of functioning alveoli. As this would be halved in the event of a pneumonectomy, the KCO is calculated to correct for lung volume. One exception is acute pulmonary haemorrhage. The reduction in lung volume causes some reduction in TLCO. However, gas exchange appears artificially good due to the increased binding of CO to the haemoglobin within the alveolar sacs, causing a high KCO. Pneumonectomy also causes a high KCO but not immediately.

Theme: Diagnosis of common congenital diseases in children

136. E

Congenital hypothyroidism is a rare but treatable cause of learning difficulties. There may be features similar to adult hypothyroidism (dry skin and hair, hyporeflexia, bradycardia, constipation and sleepiness). Neonatal features include prolonged jaundice, umbilical hernia, large protruding tongue and a flattened nasal bridge. Diagnosis is usually made by routine screening of blood collected by heel-prick in the first week. The blood is absorbed onto filter paper and tested for thyroxine and also for evidence of phenylketonuria (both congenital conditions in which early treatment may prevent the development of complications).

137. B

Sickle cell anaemia is usually suspected and identified early in childhood. It may even be identified prenatally by amniocentesis or chorionic villus sampling. As well as the typical painful thrombotic crises, children also experience dactylitis (hand and foot crisis), aplastic crises, sequestration crises and girdle syndromes. FBC will show anaemia and reticulocytosis. Blood film will show sickled and nucleated red cells and target cells. Haemoglobin electrophoresis or genetic testing gives the definitive diagnosis. Treat with analgesia, fluids, oxygen and, in some cases, exchange transfusion.

138. D

Cystic fibrosis is the commonest serious genetic condition in children in the UK (haemochromatosis is probably more common but only presents in adulthood). Diagnosis may be made with prenatal genetic testing if parents are known carriers. About 15% of children are born with meconium ileus, allowing for neonatal diagnosis to be made. The remainder develops respiratory problems and/or malabsorption with growth delay in the first few years of life. Most cases may be diagnosed with genetic testing but there are numerous possible genetic mutations, some of which have yet to be identified. A positive sweat test (sweat sodium level >60 mmol/l) is diagnostic. Respiratory infections are often due to organisms that are unusual in children – *Staph. aureus*, *Haemophilus influenzae* or *Pseudomonas aeruginosa*.

139. G

Menarche may occur as young as 8 and as old as 16 in normal girls. Primary amenorrhoea should not be diagnosed until at least the age of 16, unless there are other features of delayed sexual development such as failure of breast or pubic hair growth. Turner's syndrome (45-XO) almost always causes short stature and this may be the only feature. Diagnosis is with karyotyping from a blood sample, although absence of Barr bodies in a buccal smear is also diagnostic. Amenorrhoea is due to failure of gonadal development and is, therefore, untreatable. Growth may be improved with growth hormone if given early.

140. C

Gilbert's syndrome is a very common inherited condition that affects up to 2% of the population, many of whom remain unaware of this. Impairment of bile salt conjugation causes pre-hepatic jaundice, worse when there is physiological stress. Jaundice is only ever mild and there are no long-term complications or associations. Diagnosis is suspected by demonstrating an unconjugated (indirect) hyperbilirubinaemia in the absence of haemolysis. Formal diagnosis may be made by demonstrating a 50% rise in unconjugated bilirubin after a calorie-restricted diet or after administration of intravenous nicotinic acid. This is rarely necessary. Most other congenital causes of jaundice produce conjugated (direct) hyperbilirubinaemia and are associated with other symptoms and complications.

141. B

β Thalassaemia major is usually diagnosed in the first year of life. Children are severely anaemic and fail to thrive without treatment. The neonate is unaffected, as fetal haemoglobin (HBF – $\alpha_2\gamma_2$) does not contain β chains. If the anaemia is not treated adequately, there is expansion of haemopoietic tissue in the marrow of long bones, spine and skull, and in the liver and spleen. If the anaemia is treated, prognosis is better but limited by iron overload causing death due to cardiac haemosiderosis within the first few decades. Diagnosis is with haemoglobin electrophoresis, which shows absence of HbA, high levels of HbF and variable levels of HbA$_2$ ($\alpha_2\delta_2$).

Theme: Management of lower limb fractures

142. D

Almost all patients with a fracture of the proximal femur should have surgical treatment to allow early mobilisation and pain control. The only exceptions are patients who are clearly pre-terminal and those who were previously chair or bed-bound, as these groups of patients may not benefit from surgery. The risk of morbidity and mortality associated with prolonged bed rest is almost always higher than the risk of anaesthesia and surgery. The orthopaedic management of an intertrochanteric fracture is to use a sliding (dynamic) hip screw or an intramedullary nail with a screw through the fracture into the femoral head. The dynamic hip screw is the more common treatment.

143. L

Pubic ramus fractures rarely require operative treatment except if there is pelvic instability or associated displaced acetabular fracture, both of which are rare. Patients should be encouraged to mobilise actively as pain allows. Adequate analgesia should be provided to facilitate this. As with femoral neck fractures, the principle of treatment is to avoid prolonged bed rest.

144. H

Fractures of the ankle usually require operative treatment if there is significant disruption of the joint or if there is instability. If both malleoli are involved and the fibula is fractured at or above the tibio-fibular ligament (also called the syndesmosis) then surgical plating of the fibula is required. If there is a significant medial malleolar fragment then this should also be fixed with a screw or wire. Displaced stable fractures can be treated with closed reduction and a plaster. Non-displaced, stable fractures may only require a plaster.

145. A

Femoral shaft fractures usually follow high velocity trauma in young patients, particularly common in motorbike accidents. Patients are often shocked and fat embolism may occur. Internal fixation or traction may be used to immobilise the fracture. Risk of infection is high with open fractures if they are managed with internal fixation. Conservative treatment is favoured in open or distal fractures, and in children.

146. G

A sub-capital fracture of the femoral neck may be associated with damage to the joint capsule, resulting in impairment of the blood supply of the femoral head and subsequent avascular necrosis. If the fracture is impacted or minimally displaced (Garden grades 1 and 2), the blood supply is likely to be intact and internal fixation with cannulated screws may be used. If there is moderate or complete displacement (Garden grades 3 and 4), the blood supply is more likely to be impaired. In this case, the options are to try fixation with screws (with an appreciable risk of need for a hip replacement for avascular necrosis) or to proceed to arthroplasty. Hemi-arthroplasty is quicker and associated with fewer peri-operative complications and is favoured in older, frailer patients. Total hip replacement gives better long-term results but takes longer and has a higher rate of early complications. It is the definitive treatment for younger, fitter patients. This is a controversial area.

Theme: Management of renal failure

147. I

Hyperkalaemia is common in renal failure and may respond to a change in dialysis regime and withdrawal of contributory drugs. In mild cases ($K^+ > 5.5$–6.0 mmol/l asymptomatic), calcium resonium given orally or rectally will reduce potassium levels slowly. In moderate cases ($K^+ > 6.5$ mmol/l), patients should receive an infusion of dextrose and insulin as well as calcium resonium. In severe cases ($K^+ > 7.0$ mmol/l and/or ECG changes) the patient requires intravenous calcium chloride or gluconate to stabilise the myocardium, plus a bolus of 50 ml 50% dextrose and 10–15 units soluble insulin. The management given above then follows this.

148. G

In older men, a common cause of acute renal failure is acute-on-chronic urinary retention. Patients do not necessarily report oliguria, as retention with overflow is also common. A distended bladder is often unrecognised if it is not specifically sought. Catheterisation and active fluid management alone may completely return the renal function to normal within a few days.

149. C

Indications for emergency dialysis (filtration if dialysis is not immediately available) are persistent hyperkalaemia, fluid overload, acidosis or pericarditis.

150. A

Pre-renal failure is common in hospital patients due to poor oral intake and may be exacerbated by vomiting or diarrhoea. In a young patient, active fluid replacement is likely to be sufficient without the need for more aggressive management.

151. J

If a patient is in an extremely compromised state due to fluid overload, a suggested order of treatment is as follows (assuming presence of a catheter and central venous access):

Frusemide bolus

Repeat frusemide bolus, consider higher dose

Infusion of frusemide and/or dopamine

Infusion of nitrate (if systolic BP > 90)

Admission/Transfer to ITU for inotropic support, haemofiltration or dialysis

Consider venesection of a unit of blood in exceptional circumstances

Theme: Side-effects of medications

152. C

The use of beta-blockers is often limited by their side-effects. Fatigue and impotence, in particular, are commonly described. This certainly limits their use in the treatment of hypertension, where a patient who feels well is given medication that makes him feel unwell, rather than the other way round. In fact, impotence is a potential side-effect of most anti-hypertensives, including ACE inhibitors, thiazide diuretics and some calcium channel blockers (e.g. nifedipine and amlodipine). It is quite likely that, in many cases, the main cause for erectile dysfunction is the hypertension and not the drug. Alpha-blockers may rarely cause priapism.

153. A

Amiodarone is prone to cause many adverse effects, which limits the use of an otherwise versatile anti-arrhythmic. It may affect many organs:

Thyroid: hyperthyroidism, hypothyroidism (both common)
Lungs: alveolitis, fibrosis, pneumonitis
Liver: jaundice, hepatitis, cirrhosis, raised transaminases
Nervous system: nightmares, neuropathy, headache, ataxia, tremor
Musculoskeletal: myopathy, arthralgia
Eyes: reversible corneal microdeposits, optic neuritis (rare)
Skin: photosensitivity, dermatitis, persistent slate-grey discoloration (rare)
Heart: bradycardia, conduction disturbances

154. G

L-Dopa-containing drugs often cause gastro-intestinal disturbance, particularly nausea, which may be minimised by taking the tablets on a full stomach. Urine and other body fluids may be stained red. Cardiovascular effects include postural hypotension, which may limit the dose that the patient will tolerate (severe postural hypotension should raise the possibility of multi-system atrophy as a cause of Parkinsonism and autonomic failure). Neurological side-effects may occur early (dizziness, agitation and insomnia) or late (dyskinesias, psychosis and hallucinosis). Dyskinesias may occur with peak L-Dopa levels or with 'wearing-off'.

155. I

Thirst, polyuria, fine tremor and weight gain are common side-effects of lithium. Lithium may induce nephrogenic diabetes insipidus after prolonged usage. Patients may develop goitre with lithium and some will go on to become hypothyroid. Lithium is reabsorbed in the kidney by the same mechanism as sodium and water. Patients may develop lithium toxicity if they become dehydrated or hyponatraemic. Early lithium toxicity causes coarse tremor, agitation and twitching. Later features are coma, convulsions, arrhythmias and renal failure. Treatment is supportive with hydration and anti-convulsants as required. Dialysis is occasionally needed in severe cases.

156. D

Nausea and gastro-intestinal upset are common, non-specific side-effects of carbimazole. Rashes and pruritus are also quite common and are allergic in origin. A patient who develops a rash should be changed to propylthiouracil. Agranulocytosis and neutropenia is a rare idiosyncratic reaction to carbimazole. Patients should be specifically counselled to report any sign of infection immediately, especially a sore throat, and have an urgent full blood count. Agranulocytosis is reversible on stopping the drug.

Theme: Causes of clubbing

Most cases of clubbing are hereditary, congenital or idiopathic.

157. I

Infective endocarditis is easily overlooked as a cause of sub-acute or chronic illness in older people. However, fever and murmurs often coexist without endocarditis. Endocarditis on a previously normal valve is more common after surgical instrumentation of the urogenital or gastro-intestinal tract or after dental work. Clinical signs include clubbing, splinter haemorrhages, haematuria, retinal Roth spots (basically cotton wool spots due to vasculitis), Janeway lesions (palmar macules) and Osler's nodes (painful papules on the finger pulps).

158. D

Any chronic suppurative lung disease can cause clubbing. In a young or middle-aged person, the most likely diagnosis is bronchiectasis. This may be idiopathic or follow previous infection (whooping cough, TB) or bronchial obstruction, which causes localised bronchiectasis. Signs are due to fixed narrowing of some airways with excess sputum production. In a younger patient, cystic fibrosis gives a similar clinical picture, including clubbing.

159. A

Most lung malignancies are associated with clubbing apart from small cell bronchial carcinoma. Asbestos exposure is a risk factor for both mesothelioma and bronchial carcinoma. Smoking and asbestos exposure together massively increase the risk of lung malignancy. Squamous cell carcinoma is more common than mesothelioma and Horner's syndrome is usually due to an apical squamous cell cancer.

160. F

Cystic fibrosis, coeliac disease and Crohn's disease can all cause malabsorption, growth delay and clubbing. Of these, coeliac is the most common condition to present at this age. Cystic fibrosis is almost always identified in young children and most will have respiratory problems at the time of diagnosis. Children with coeliac disease are often pale skinned with fair hair. Arthralgia and dermatitis herpetiformis may also occur.

161. L

Unilateral clubbing is rare. One cause is an axillary artery aneurysm, which is usually acquired in adulthood after trauma such as angiography via the brachial artery. Another possibility is coarctation of the aorta proximal to the origin of the right subclavian artery. Clubbing usually involves the toes as well as the fingers; these examples are exceptions to this rule.

Theme: Advice for travellers – malaria prophylaxis

As with travel immunisations, expert advice should be sought in any case where the prophylactic regime is unclear. Travellers must also take steps to avoid mosquito bites – e.g. mosquito nets, sprays or lotions, long sleeved shirts and trousers after dusk.

162. A

Most Caribbean countries are not malarial and no prophylaxis is required. You should, however, check that this traveller is remaining in Jamaica and does not intend to watch cricket in Guyana also. In which case, he might need to take mefloquine.

163. E

The borders of Thailand and Cambodia are one of the few places where Doxycycline is recommended for malaria prophylaxis, even though it is not licensed for this use. The other places are Papua New Guinea, the Solomon Islands and Vanuatu. Seek expert advice.

164. C

Previous malaria confers no protection against subsequent infection. It is not uncommon for people travelling between the UK and a malarial country to neglect their malarial prophylaxis, despite a history of the illness. Chloroquine resistance is high in most of Sub-Saharan Africa and southeast Asia, so mefloquine is the prophylactic treatment of choice.

165. F

Mefloquine is highly effective in prophylaxis against chloroquine-resistant falciparum malaria. Adverse events are common and may be serious or irreversible, which has led to much publicity. Of particular concern is the risk of neuropsychiatric effects, including neuropathies, agitation, anxiety, depression, hallucinations and psychosis, which occur in around 1/1000 people. There is often reluctance amongst travellers to take the drug, even though the risk to their health from malaria is probably greater. Mefloquine is contraindicated in anyone with a history of neuropsychiatric illness, including depression and convulsions. The risk of malaria in coastal Kenya is quite low and prophylaxis with chloroquine and proguanil is a reasonable alternative for this traveller.

Theme: Investigation of lumps in the neck

166. E

Unilateral parotid swelling is usually due to a pleomorphic adenoma (mixed parotid tumour). It may be indistinguishable from carcinoma clinically, although carcinoma is usually painful, rapidly growing and may cause facial nerve palsy. Excision biopsy provides diagnosis and treatment. Incomplete biopsy may seed the tumour in the wound.

167. I

A pulsatile mass in the neck is either due to a carotid artery aneurysm or a carotid body tumour (chemodectoma). The latter is usually firm but may be soft and pulsatile. Diagnosis may be made with Doppler ultrasound or digital subtraction angiography, which is the more discriminatory test. Do not go anywhere near these masses with a needle!

168. D

A solitary thyroid nodule may be benign or malignant; secreting or non-secreting; solid or cystic; and may be 'hot' or 'cold' (depending on uptake of radiolabelled iodine). Many cold nodules are malignant but may be non-secreting adenomas. Hot nodules are usually adenomas but may rarely be follicular carcinomas. On ultrasound, cystic nodules are usually benign, solid ones may be malignant. No single radiological investigation is diagnostic. Tissue diagnosis is required for any nodule unless it is hot and cystic, or the patient is thyrotoxic. Therefore the most discriminatory test is fine needle aspiration for cytology. Proceeding straight to excision biopsy will mean that many benign lesions are removed unnecessarily and that some malignant lesions are not excised completely.

169. A

Multinodular goitre may occur in association with hyperthyroidism or, rarely, hypothyroidism. It is most commonly associated with a euthyroid state. Ultrasound will confirm the typical multinodular architecture to make the diagnosis. Multiple nodules do not require histological investigation, as they are almost never malignant. Thyroid function tests will help guide treatment.

170. J

Salivary gland stones most commonly occur in the submandibular gland. The clinical picture as given is classical. The stone may be palpable if it is in the duct. Confirmation of the diagnosis is made with plain X-ray or contrast sialography. Stones in the duct may be expressed bimanually; stones in the gland may require surgical excision.

171. K

Cervical lymphadenopathy may be the first and only clinical sign of an underlying carcinoma of the pharynx, larynx, head or neck. Any lymph node that cannot be otherwise explained must be investigated with this in mind. Direct nasopharyngoscopy should be performed as a bare minimum in order to identify any mucosal lesions. Occasionally the diagnosis may only be made after node biopsy reveals metastatic squamous cell carcinoma but the underlying cause is usually visible, if it is looked for.

Theme: Investigation of hyperventilation

172. C

Hyperventilation can be a physiological response to metabolic acidosis. This may be due to an excess of endogenous acid (e.g. lactic or keto acids) or exogenous acid (such as occurs in poisoning with methanol, ethylene glycol or salicylate). Salicylates are commonly used for self-harm, as they are freely available over the counter. Salicylates may cause a number of acid-base disturbances including metabolic acidosis (due to organic acid), respiratory alkalosis (as a response to metabolic acidosis) or respiratory acidosis (due to respiratory depression – a late and serious sign). Tinnitus is relatively specific for salicylate poisoning.

173. F

A number of major complications may occur after long bone fracture, all of which may present with hyperventilation: pneumonia is common and usually occurs during the first week as a consequence of immobility and hypoventilation, caused by the injury and analgesia. Pulmonary embolism classically occurs around days 7 to 10 after injury or surgery but can occur at any time. A deep vein thrombosis is easily missed in a fractured limb. Uraemia and renal failure may occur secondary to myoglobinuria if there is extensive muscle damage and rhabdomyolysis. Acute tubular necrosis may also occur in response to toxins released from ischaemia of other soft tissues. Fat embolism is a specific complication of long bone trauma and presents between the 3rd and 10th days with collapse, confusion, fits, coma, hypoxia, dyspnoea, fever and a petechial rash. There is no specific diagnostic test for fat embolism, the diagnosis being made clinically. Severe hypoxia is supportive of the diagnosis and excludes some of the differentials.

174. H

Diabetic ketoacidosis may occur as a first presentation of diabetes or as a complication in a known diabetic. Early symptoms of diabetes include thirst, polydipsia, polyuria, weight loss, fatigue and blurred vision. Ketoacidosis may develop rapidly over a period of hours. The smell of ketones may be identified on the patient's breath, but some people are congenitally unable to smell ketones. The diagnosis of diabetic ketoacidosis requires the presence of hyperglycaemia, ketones and acidosis. It is quite common for a patient with diabetes to become hyperglycaemic and ketotic, without acidosis, after a period of vomiting or poor calorie intake. The blood glucose is the best test to distinguish between other causes of a metabolic acidosis.

175. B

Rigors only occur in a limited number of infections commonly found in the UK: lobar pneumonia, pyelonephritis, cholangitis, empyema (of any organ) and some abscesses. Worldwide, malaria and typhoid fever are very common causes of rigors and should not be forgotten if there is a history of travel. Delirium, acute confusional state, may occur with a severe infection in a young person, particularly if there is also hypoxia. If the cause is pneumonia, the clinical and radiological features should confirm this. If the clinical signs and chest X-ray fail to confirm the diagnosis, then another cause for the rigors should be sought.

176. J

The question strongly hints at a hereditary disease. A sickle cell crisis is the obvious and correct choice. The patient may have a chest crisis, which is a medical emergency and is usually an indication for an exchange transfusion. Hyperventilation may be due to pain, acidosis or hypoxia. Cyanosis is rare, as it is easy for haemoglobin to be fully saturated if a patient is anaemic. Blood gases will reveal a low pO_2 despite the normal O_2 saturation. The patient urgently requires analgesia, fluids (to correct the acidosis) and oxygen (to correct the hypoxia). Full blood count and film will diagnose the underlying disease and quantify the degree of anaemia.

177. E

Sudden collapse in pregnancy may be due to shock (e.g. uterine rupture or ante-partum haemorrhage from placenta praevia or abruption); hypoxia (e.g. pulmonary or amniotic fluid embolism); sepsis or eclampsia. All of these conditions may cause hyperventilation. Hyperventilation without collapse is very common in pregnant women, due to physiological changes. In this instance, the most likely cause of collapse with hypoxia and shock is a pulmonary embolism. The differential diagnosis would include amniotic fluid embolism, eclampsia and sepsis. Spiral CT chest with contrast will show filling defects. An echocardiogram will usually diagnose a major pulmonary embolism but is less sensitive than CT. Pulmonary angiography is the gold standard but is limited by its availability and risk of complications. The patient is too unwell for a ventilation-perfusion scan.

Theme: Warnings for specific drugs

178. F

Sulfasalazine has many potential side-effects. Serious ones include anaemia, Stevens-Johnson syndrome, oligospermia and renal problems. Urine and tears may be coloured orange and this may cause staining of soft contact lenses. Photosensitivity also occurs rarely. Other drugs that colour the urine include rifampicin (red), L-dopa (dark red), triamterene (blue) and phenolphthalein (pink if urine is alkaline).

179. C

Chlorpropamide is rarely used nowadays due to its long duration of action and greater risk of side-effects than other sulphonylureas. It has a greater risk of hypoglycaemia than shorter acting agents. When taken with alcohol it may cause unpleasant flushing, an effect that does not occur with other sulphonylureas. Other drugs that often cause flushing with alcohol are metronidazole and disulfiram and patients should be specifically advised about this.

180. I

Sildenafil is a vasodilator and often causes flushing and headaches. A rare occurrence is that patients notice a bluish tinge to their vision. This is due to the effect of sildenafil, a phosphodiesterase inhibitor, on phosphodiesterase in the retina. Another drug that causes change in colour perception is digoxin, which causes a yellow tinge if the drug is at toxic levels.

181. G

Alendronate is associated with a risk of oesophageal spasm, pain, ulcers and strictures. Patients may reduce this risk by following the advice given in the question. This certainly limits compliance with an otherwise useful drug. Patients should also be warned to stop the drug and seek medical attention if they develop oesophageal symptoms.

182. H

Ampicillin and other broad-spectrum antibiotics may cause reduced oral contraceptive efficacy. This is due to the loss of bowel flora that normally recycle ethinyloestradiol from the large bowel. The risk is relatively small but patients should use barrier methods during the course of antibiotics and for a week afterwards. Rifampicin, on the other hand, is a potent hepatic enzyme inducer and almost certainly renders standard dose contraceptives useless.

Theme: Causes of hepatomegaly

183. D

Glandular fever (infectious mononucleosis) may cause liver or spleen enlargement in around 10% of cases. Occasionally the organs are painful due to rapid expansion causing stretching of the capsule. Rarely, splenic enlargement may be so rapid that the spleen is liable to rupture. LFTs are often deranged but rarely checked.

184. F

Liver metastases commonly arise from bowel and breast. Palpable metastases need not have any effect on liver function, which is only impaired if the metastases involve over half the liver or if there is biliary obstruction.

185. A

Right heart failure is often forgotten as a cause of ascites and hepatomegaly, due to congestive changes. In tricuspid regurgitation, the enlarged liver may be pulsatile. The commonest causes of right heart failure are left heart failure, hypertension and valvular disease. Rheumatic fever rarely causes tricuspid or pulmonary valve lesions, so this patient probably has cardiac failure that is primarily due to aortic or mitral valve disease or hypertension.

186. L

Patients with chronic inflammatory diseases may develop secondary amyloidosis. Causative conditions include rheumatoid arthritis, bronchiectasis and chronic osteomyelitis. Amyloid accumulates in lymphoreticular and other tissues, such as the tongue and skin. Purpura may be due to cutaneous amyloid or hypersplenism-induced thrombocytopenia. Cardiac amyloid is rare in secondary amyloid. Felty's syndrome is the main differential diagnosis in a patient with hepatosplenomegaly and rheumatoid arthritis.

187. J

Patients with lymphoma may either present with a lump (or lumps) or with generalised symptoms. Of particular importance are 'B symptoms' – weight loss, fever, night sweats – which affect the choice of treatment and prognosis of the disease. Involvement of extra-nodal sites, such as liver, spleen and bone marrow, puts this patient at stage 4B. This is the highest stage and carries the worst prognosis. Treatment is chemotherapy after histological confirmation. Lymph node pain on drinking alcohol is said to be a feature of Hodgkin's disease.

Theme: Causes of pulmonary oedema

188. E

Pulmonary oedema may occur in the presence of normal left ventricular function if there is high left atrial pressure, as occurs with mitral stenosis. Mitral stenosis should be suspected in any older patient with a history of recurrent episodes of pulmonary oedema and little evidence of left ventricular disease. The murmur may not be audible but a history of rheumatic fever and the presence of a tapping apex or loud first heart sound should point to the diagnosis. Episodes of paroxysmal atrial fibrillation may be the cause of the recurring pulmonary oedema.

189. H

Fluid overload is a common cause of pulmonary oedema in hospital and may occur in the absence of a previous history of cardiac disease. It is thought that hypoxia and hypotension, possibly related to anaesthetic and analgesic agents, cause ischaemia of the myocardium and underperfusion of the kidneys. This leads to oliguria, fluid retention and impaired cardiac output resulting in pulmonary oedema usually on the second or third day after surgery.

190. B

Pulmonary oedema of cardiac origin is unusual in younger patients with no previous cardiac history. Myocardial infarction may rarely occur in a young patient with diabetes, familial hyper-cholesterolaemia, and congenitally anomalous coronary arteries or after abuse of cocaine. Myocarditis is a more common, but still rare, cause of acute cardiac failure in a young person. The history is usually longer and less acute than a myocardial infarction and there are usually symptoms of infection such as fever. Signs of right heart failure often predominate initially. Recognised causes include Coxsackie virus, diphtheria, HIV, toxoplasma and group A streptococcus (rheumatic fever). Treatment is supportive but patients may require inotropic drugs, ventricular assist devices or even transplantation.

191. J

Adult respiratory distress syndrome (ARDS) is acute severe pulmonary oedema due to acute capillary leakage in response to severe illness or trauma. It is usually part of a more generalised multi-organ failure and has a mortality approaching 50%. The following is needed to make the diagnosis:

An underlying cause for ARDS
Bilateral pulmonary oedema on chest X-ray
Persistent hypoxia despite inspired oxygen concentration > 40%
Normal or near-normal capillary wedge pressure (i.e. not cardiac failure)
Normal oncotic pressure (not due to severe hypoalbuminaemia)
Poor lung compliance (stiff lungs, possibly due to endothelial damage)

In this patient with acute pancreatitis, pulmonary oedema may be due to fluid overload but this is unlikely if the urine output is good. Hypoalbuminaemia is also a common complication of pancreatitis but levels well below 30 mmol/l are required before significant oedema develops.

Theme: Treatment of psychiatric disease

192. C

This patient has depression with biological features and suicidal ideation. There is also a suggestion that she may have mood-congruent delusions regarding her boss and auditory hallucinations that pre-date the loss of her job. It is equally possible that her boss did indeed record her calls and think that she was a bad worker. In either case, there is good evidence for a diagnosis of major depression, possibly with psychosis. This requires treatment, ideally on a voluntary outpatient basis. Any anti-depressant may be given but SSRIs are favoured for their relative lack of side-effects and greater safety in overdose.

193. F

This is a not uncommon scenario of acute psychosis, probably in a patient with a long history of chronic schizophrenia. It could also be a manic psychosis. The patient clearly lacks capacity for rational decision-making and may be a risk to himself or others. Formal detention in hospital under the Mental Health Act (1983) section 2 allows for a 28-day period of assessment. He will require medication with a neuroleptic agent to permit this. Haloperidol, droperidol and chlorpromazine are all commonly used for initial management of acute psychosis.

194. L

After childbirth, mothers often experience low mood due to a combination of psychological and neuro-endocrine changes. 'Baby blues' are common, mild and self-limiting. Post-natal depression may be more serious and associated with biological features. It too is often self-limiting and requires supportive psychological treatments in the first instance. Anti-depressants may be required in more severe, prolonged cases. Puerperal psychosis is less common (1/500 live births) and associated with severe mood disturbance, attempts to harm mother and/or baby, and delusions of malformations in a normal baby. This requires in-patient treatment in a specialised mother and baby unit.

195. J

Behavioural problems in a person with dementia should be managed with caution. It is important to be clear whether you are giving treatment for their benefit, or for the benefit of carers and other observers of the behaviour. If a patient is not distressed or at risk of harm, they should not be given medication, particularly if they are at risk of falls. Visual hallucinations and severe agitation do warrant medication, provided it is used with care and monitored closely. Neuroleptic agents are usually effective but may be limited by extra-pyramidal side-effects or sedation. Newer anti-psychotic drugs, such as risperidone and olanzapine, cause fewer extra-pyramidal effects and would be favoured for this patient. The patient in this question has a combination of dementia, visual hallucinations, behavioural problems and Parkinsonism, which suggests a diagnosis of Lewy body dementia.

Theme: Investigation of malignant disease

196. F

Investigation of a breast lump includes mammography and/or ultrasound and either fine needle aspiration, incision (Tru-cut) biopsy or excision biopsy. If a patient has a strong family history, some form of cytological or histological specimen will be required before a diagnosis of malignancy is excluded. Mammography is often unreliable in women with lumpy breasts or in younger women. Ultrasound is useful for cystic lesions in particular. Fine needle aspiration for cytology may be performed in clinic; biopsy may not always be possible in an outpatient setting.

197. I

Testicular swellings are usually benign cysts but ultrasound is needed to exclude solid tumours. Previous non-descent of a testis (treated with orchidopexy) is a risk factor for testicular malignancy. Diagnosis cannot be made without histology but testicular ultrasound must be performed first to avoid unnecessary removal of a normal testis.

198. G

Prostatic symptoms are usually due to benign hypertrophy rather than malignant disease. PSA is raised in most cases of prostate cancer, but may also be moderately raised in benign disease or following rectal examination. Histology is important to make the diagnosis and guide treatment. It is usual to obtain multiple histology specimens by trans-rectal incision biopsy.

199. L

CEA is associated with bowel cancer but with low sensitivity and specificity. If a patient with primary bowel cancer has an elevated CEA, the CEA may be used to screen for early recurrence. As we do not know whether the CEA was previously raised, a normal CEA may be a false negative. Colonoscopy is needed to investigate for recurrence, particularly in light of her new symptoms.

200. I

CA 19-9 is a tumour marker that is raised in ovarian carcinoma. It is non-specific and is often elevated in ascites due to other malignancies or cirrhosis. The investigation of choice is an abdominal ultrasound to confirm the presence of ascites and look for evidence of ovarian masses. Cytology of the ascites, if positive, may be diagnostic but is often unrewarding.

APPENDIX 1

In the July 2000 Part 1 exam candidates were provided with a booklet containing normal values for all tests. Below is a short list of normal values as applied to the exam in this book:

Biochemistry

Sodium	135–145 mmol/l
Potassium	3.5–4.8 mmol/l
Urea	2.5–6.7 mmol/l
Creatinine	50–110 μmol/l
Glucose	3.5–5.5 mmol/l
HbA1c	< 7% indicates reasonable glucose control
Bilirubin	3–17 mmol/l
Alanine aminotransferase	5–35 iu/l
Alkaline phosphatase	30–150 iu/l (varies between hospitals)
Calcium (total)	2.12–2.65 mmol/l
Phosphate	0.8–1.45 mmol/l
C-reactive protein	<10 iu/l
Total cholesterol	<5.2 mmol/l (lower if high cardiovascular risk)
Triglyceride (fasting)	<2.3 mmol/l

Arterial blood gases

pH	7.35–7.45
pCO_2	4.7–6.0 kPa
pO_2	>10.6 kPa
Bicarbonate	24–30 mmol/l
O_2 saturation	> 97%

Haematology

Haemoglobin (Hb)	male	13.5–18.0 g/dl
	female	11.5–16.0 g/dl
White cell count (WCC)		4.0–11.0 x 10^9/ml
Platelets		150–400 x 10^9/l
Mean corpuscular volume (MCV)		78–96 fl
Mean corpuscular haemoglobin (MCH)		27–32 pg
Red cell count	male	4.5–6.5 x 10^{12}/l
	female	3.9–5.6 x 10^{12}/l
ESR		< 20 mm/hr
HbA_2		<3%

APPENDIX 2

A number of drugs are known by different names in the UK to other countries, particularly the USA. Spellings often differ from accepted international spellings. Many of the British Approved Names are to be changed in line with the Recommended International Non-proprietary Names. There are a number of exceptions where the British name or spelling is so well established that either name may be used interchangeably. A few British names have been retained for drugs used in emergency settings, where confusion might be dangerous. In this book, I have mostly used the International name, except for emergency drugs. The lists below are not exhaustive but cover most drugs in common use. A full list may be found in the British National Formulary (BNF).

Drugs where the British name has been retained

British Approved Name	Recommended International Non-proprietary Name
adrenaline	epinephrine
bendrofluazide	bendroflumethiazide
chlorpheniramine	chlorphenamine
frusemide	furosemide
lignocaine	lidocaine
methylene blue	methylthioninium chloride
noradrenaline	norepinephrine

Drugs where the British spelling remains in common usage

British Approved Name	Recommended International Non-proprietary Name
amoxycillin	amoxicillin
beclomethasone	beclometasone
cephalexin	cefalexin
chlormethiazole	clomethiazole
cholecalciferol	colecalciferol
cholestyramine	colestyramine
corticotrophin	corticotropin
indomethacin	indometacin
phenobarbitone	phenobarbital
sodium cromoglycate	sodium cromoglicate
sulphasalazine	sulfasalazine

INDEX

Index

PASTEST REVISION COURSES FOR
<u>PLAB PART 1</u>

Feeling in need of a helping hand towards success in your exams?

PasTest has over thirty years' experience in helping doctors to pass first time, with specially tailored courses to make the most of your valuable revision time.

To give you the most up-to-date information and help you to achieve the best results, we constantly update and improve our courses based on feedback from those who attend.

Our course is run by Consultants and Senior Registrars from leading London teaching hospitals, who have extensive knowledge of their specialty.

Our course material is continually updated to ensure the best possible revision for the exam. You will also receive a complete EMQ mock exam, with explanations and detailed handouts.

- **Course Content**
  Our teaching sessions are based around the PLAB Part 1 examination. The course covers core knowledge, skills and attitudes relating to all exam topics including: Accident and Emergency, Surgery, Medicine, Paediatrics, Obstetrics and Gynaecology, Trauma and Orthopaedics. Our course material includes EMQs with answers and teaching notes, an EMQ examination, tips on examination technique, detailed lecture notes for each subject and a recommended reading list.

For priority mail order service, please contact PasTest on 01565 752000, or ORDER ONLINE AT OUR SECURE WEBSITE

PasTest Ltd, Egerton Court, Parkgate Estate, Knutsford, Cheshire WA16 8DX
Telephone: 01565 752000   Fax: 01565 650264
E-mail: books@pastest.co.uk   Website: http//www.pastest.co.uk